Acting Out the Gospels

with MIMES PUPPETS & CLOWNS

William DeAngelis

ST. THOMAS SCHOOL

D1604772

TWENTY-THIRD PUBLICATIONS
P.O. Box 180 Mystic, CT 06355

DEDICATION

In Loving Memory

Rev. Raymond William Gribbin

Pastor, St. Joseph Church

February 20, 1924 - October 28, 1981

He introduced me to the love and joy of children.
I called him Pastor; he called me Friend.

ISBN 0-89622-136-9

Library of Congress Card Cataloging Number 81-84919

Cover design by Robert Maitland
Book design by John G. van Bemmel
Edited by Maureen Geruth

Preface

Welcome to the land of children and youth. It's the kind of place one loves to visit—and wants to live there too. I've been living here for several years now. I've never been so happy, so full of joy, so impulsive. Children hold a secret of life they cannot verbalize; they're too busy living it. If you can raise yourself to their level of understanding, if you can set aside some of your inhibitions, if you can dare to be spontaneous, you'll begin, (just begin, mind you) to know their secret. And that is what these pages are all about.

If you've come here to read about children's liturgy theories, philosophies, or theologies, you're in the wrong place. This is not a reading book; it's a doing book. If you "do" just one of these children's liturgies, you'll be as hooked as I am. We at St. Joseph's Church in Fullerton, Maryland began celebrating our children with a puppet liturgy. We were thrilled beyond expectations when 80 children came. Our second children's liturgy was attended by over 250 children with over 700 adults (who became children at heart). And now, several years later, a total attendance of less than 1000 is unusual.

After studying the outline format, the scripts, and the appendix you'll note a simplicity that runs throughout. If I've come to realize one thing about children's liturgies it is, the simpler they are, the better they are. And with children, simple also means short. I've seen what works from experience: make them loud, full of music, full of colors, full of action, get in quickly, make your point, and get out. I see my job as one of creating an atmosphere for the child to have an experience of God (and this is nothing unusual for a child). If it enhances the liturgy, use it.

You'll also note a similarity in the props called for in the scripts. Simplicity again. Basically, I'm lazy. So I use props that can be used over and over again. Some need small changes, some need different colors and some work well as they are. The scripts are written for someone who is busy and involved in other things. Necessity is the mother of invention for these scripts.

I offer this liturgy program not as ideas conceived in a backroom from a night of inspiration. But rather, I offer the program as liturgies that reek of sweat and are soiled from use. They were discussed, written, rewritten, performed, observed, and rewritten again. They have the "bugs" ironed out of them. They are as short as they can be and have proven to be successful.

The joy that spontaneous and impulsive youngsters bring to their celebration if they like and understand it is almost overwhelming. And through the years, I've come to know that God smiles a lot. He has smiled on me and has blessed me with hundreds of beautiful children. I feel privileged to be able to introduce them to something they have shown me—God's love and joy.

William J. DeAngelis

Contents

Planning a Successful Liturgy

More than a week before the liturgy, develop an insert announcing the young people's liturgy for the Sunday bulletin. Distribute this one week prior to the Mass. See Appendix.

Develop an invitation to be handed out to all the school and CCD children up to the eighth grade. These should be distributed during the last day of classes just before the liturgy. See Appendix.

On the day of the liturgy, rehearse the songs to be used with the children and adults present. If there are any songs to be used that encourage hand motions, explain and rehearse them thoroughly. Try to use the same songs as much as possible liturgy after liturgy. Let the school and CCD be aware of the songs well in advance so they may practice during classes. A lay person should read the normal Sunday announcements.

Announce that every child should come down the aisle at Communion time. If they have not made their First Communion, they should place their finger over their mouth. If this is the case, then the Minister of the Eucharist will lay a hand upon the child's head and ask Jesus to bless him or her. This should be stated again by the celebrant just prior to Communion distribution: "We want every child here to receive Jesus either in the Eucharist or in his blessing." Great care should be used to explain this to the children; many kids make their First Communion at this time if the procedure is not explained well. Special announcements should be made last; for example, that you are having a Bread Festival for the children after Mass, if the festival happens to be on the theme of Eucharist.

INTRODUCTORY RITE

Entrance Ask the adults to remain seated during the entrance procession so that the children may see what happens or see one another while singing and doing the hand participation songs. (Several excellent songs are found in the *Hi God* albums by Carey Landry.) It is a must to open with a participating song led by your folk group; this sets the tone of the entire liturgy.

Greeting The celebrant opens with a short prayer, blessing, greeting, and theme statement. He then asks everyone to remain seated for the gospel play. He goes to the first pew to watch the gospel play with and among the children. The Penitential Rite, the Kyrie, Gloria, and Opening Prayer are usually omitted.

LITURGY OF THE WORD

First reading—none
Second reading—none
Gospel—use one of the enclosed gospel plays.

Homily
After the gospel play, the celebrant should rise and invite the boys and girls up around the altar. Once they are seated in the sanctuary, his "short and direct" homily begins. When large numbers of children are present, it is not advisable to do a question-and-answer homily. Immediately after the homily, the celebrant leads the children in a spontaneous Prayer of the Faithful (Petitions). To dismiss the children, the celebrant tells them that they are to receive a small gift before they go back to their pews. He gives them the prepared handout. (See Appendix.) The Profession of Faith is usually omitted.

THE LITURGY OF THE EUCHARIST

Preparation of the Altar and Gifts
The altar table up to this point should be bare. Those who performed in the gospel play should now set the altar table. The celebrant remains in his pew. They bring up a table cloth and place it over the altar table. They then place upon it candles, flowers, bread, and wine. It is here that the celebrant comes to the altar to receive the collection basket. Any banners to be used for this Mass should be hung now, preferably on the front of the altar table. It is very meaningful to have this narrated for the children. Then an offertory song can be sung if preferred.

Eucharistic Prayer
The celebrant should use the Bishops' Council *Eucharistic Prayer for Children II* with sung responses. Try to encourage the children to sing; they should have no time of uninvolvement. Excellent sung responses for the Eucharistic Prayer can be found in the album, *Bloom Where You Are Planted* by Cary Landry.

COMMUNION RITE

The Lord's Prayer
The celebrant should ask everyone to stand and join hands, even across the aisles, as they sing the Our Father. Again, an excellent version is found in *Bloom Where You Are Planted*.

The Sign of Peace
This is done without song or music. The folk group and celebrant should go into the aisles to shake hands with the children at their level.

Breaking Bread
Sing the "Lamb of God" while the celebrant or deacon is distributing the Body of Christ to the eucharistic ministers.

Communion
As mentioned before, it is wise to remind those children who have not made their First Communion of the special instructions for them as they come down for Jesus' blessing. A Communion song should be played, but not one that requires hand involvement. Excellent songs are those of repetition: the child repeats the song leader's line.

Meditation
None, unless time allows.

CONCLUDING RITE

Dismissal   Again, the celebrant asks the adults to be seated so that the children can see. As the singing continues the celebrant should retrieve the altar banner and carry it out holding it high for the children to see.

Special Note   At each liturgy, pick one part of the Mass and narrate it for the children. For example, just before the "Washing of the Hands" the celebrant pauses while someone explains:

Children, the next part of the Mass is called "the washing of the hands." The altar server will bring a bowl of water with a towel to Father. Long, long ago there wasn't much money around and people bought things by trading the food and animals they had. Someone might give you a sheep for a load of corn and vegetables. Well, that's how they made their donations to the church, too. They didn't have money to give so at the Offertory part of Mass they brought their gifts of animals, fruit and vegetables for the church. After Father received all their offerings, his hands would be soiled from handling everything. He washed them before he prayed over the bread and wine. He wanted to be as clean as ever when the Body and Blood of Jesus was to be present. Now, he still washes his hands, but for all of us as a symbol of our wanting to be clean in body and spirit to meet Jesus in the Eucharist.

Now the celebrant washes his hands in full view of the children. He says his prayer loud enough for all to hear.

Staging

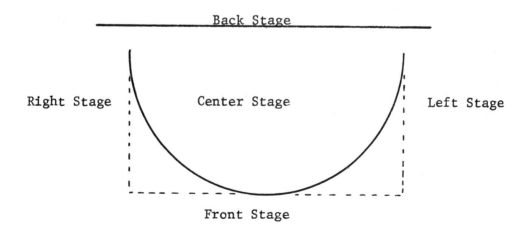

9

Super Seed

A clown mime for children adapted from Matthew 13:1 – 19

Characters   Narrator
Farmer
Hard Ground
Rocky Soil
Thorny Weeds
Good Soil
(Mimes with clown costumes and make-up)

Props   One orange shoulder bagfull of small colored balloons, and one large balloon with Super Seed face on it

Hard Ground clown backpack: 2' x 2' cardboard with several pieces of two-sided tape on it, tied on the back

Rocky Soil clown backpack: 2' x 2' cardboard with tinfoil rocks taped to it and several pieces of two-sided tape on it and tied on the back

Thorny Weeds clown backpack: 2' x 2' cardboard with green construction-paper weeds with faces, and 5 – 10 thumb tacks glued up-side down to the cardboard and tied on the back

One large brown blanket for Good Soil

One tree branch with several small colored balloons taped to its smaller twigs

One Jerusalem signpost on a stick

Staging   The stage is set with the Jerusalem signpost standing in the background and the tree branch lying at front stage.

Narrator   Let's take ourselves back across the years, way back to when Jesus was on earth. Well, here we are in the countryside near the city of Jerusalem. Just back there is Jerusalem. Isn't it beautiful out here in the country? Look over there . . .

Enter a clown, Hard Ground, from the stage right with backpack. He goes to stage left and gets down on all fours. He looks around at the chidren and mimes aloof.

Narrator   . . . there's the path where all the people walk down to Jerusalem. It's very hard ground, very hard indeed. It has to be hard to handle the thousands of donkeys, camels, and sheep that are led in and out of the city every day. As a matter of fact, it's the hardest ground around here. And over there, see, just down the path . . .

Enter one clown, Rocky Soil, from stage left with backpack. She goes to stage right and gets down on all fours. She mimes as if showing off her muscles and great strength to the children.

Narrator   . . . there's a stretch of ground with lots of rocks scattered around. Even deep down in the soil there are many rocks. It's very rocky soil. And there, toward the center, there . . .

Enter one clown, Thorny Weeds, from stage right with backpack. He goes to center stage and gets down on all fours. He mimes mean and grouchy to the children.

Narrator   . . . there's a patch of old thorny weeds. Just look how mean and nasty they look. I've never seen such long thorns before. They've been there a long time, I'm sure. No one ever walks over there; you might get stuck. Ah, and there, just beyond the thorny weeds, see?

Enter one clown, Good Soil, with the blanket wrapped around her. She enters from stage left and goes to front stage where she very obviously flings the blanket up as she lays down on her back pulling the blanket up to her neck. She rolls from side to side tucking in the blanket and faces the children as she goes to sleep.

Narrator   There's the good soil. Just look how rich and brown it is. It gets sun all the day long. When it rains, it gets all the water it could possibly need. No one walks on it because it's over beyond the thorny weeds and out of the way. It's kind of hard to get to. It looks so comfortable (yawn) it almost puts you to sleep. (Pause) Well, here we are in the Jerusalem countryside. And today is the day Jesus is telling us another story. Here is what he tells us.

Enter one clown, Farmer, from stage right throwing a few balloons from his bag as he goes over to Hard Soil at stage left.

Narrator   There was a farmer scattering seeds in his field. It was a windy day and many of the seeds took off on the wind like birds. The seeds blew every which way. One special seed got caught on the farmer's shoulder.

Farmer takes the large balloon and sticks it to a two-sided piece of tape on his shoulder. He continues casting smaller balloons.

Narrator   That seed was extra large and very strong and well-formed. It was a Super Seed. Super Seed wanted to pick where he would fall so he held on to the farmer rather than flying in the wind. All the seeds were so excited; they couldn't wait to get down to the ground so they could grow strong and healthy. Some of the seeds fell on the path where the people and animals walked, the very hard ground.

Farmer should be over to Hard Soil by now. He pushes several balloons onto the tape on the backpack. He struggles as he tries unsuccessfully to shove them through the hard soil. The Hard Soil clown looks up at him and mimes with face and one hand: "Get away; you can't come in."

Narrator The seeds skidded and slid on the hard ground. "What a rotten break," they all said. "This soil is too hard. We can't get inside to start to grow. Our food and water is down there. Help! Help! We want to come in, Mr. Hard Soil. We'll die up here."

Hard Soil shakes his head no.

Narrator The seeds saw the people and animals coming and cried louder, "Help, let us in." But Hard Soil had no soft spots. After the seeds were walked upon, the birds came and ate them all up.

Farmer throws more balloons up as he moves to Rocky Soil at stage right.

Narrator The farmer sowed more seeds to the wind. Super Seed was glad he didn't try to join the seeds that fell upon the hard soil. He was almost ready to join them when he saw the fun they had sliding along the hard surface. Now he watched the wind carry the other seeds over to the rocky soil. They looked safe, but he decided to wait.

Farmer should be next to Rocky Soil by now. He places several balloons on the tape on the backpack. Rocky Soil keeps shaking her head no.

Narrator No people walked here by the rocky soil and the seeds felt safe. They dug into the soil and took root, quickly. But just below the soil lay hundreds of rocks that wouldn't let their roots get through to the food and water. Soon the tiny green shoots began to die. They fought with the rocks to get through but the rocks were too strong. "Get out of the way, rocks," they cried. But the rocks said that this was their home and they weren't letting anyone in. These seeds dried up and died in the hot sun. Super Seed was glad he waited.

Farmer throws more balloons up as he goes to Thorny Weeds at center stage.

Narrator The farmer crisscrossed, walked up and down and all around. The sky was alive with flying seeds. Some of the seeds fell in the thorny weeds. Super Seed knew he didn't want to try to grow in there; they looked mean.

Farmer presses some balloons off to the side of the tacks on Thorny Weeds backpack. Thorny Weeds mimes very mean and scratches with one hand toward the farmer.

Some of the seeds thought they could make friends with the thorny weeds and tried to grow with them. But very soon the thorny weeds ate all the food and drank all the water. They even blocked the sun from the little seeds.

Farmer presses some balloons on the tacks surprising everyone as they burst and he jumps back. He does this several times.

Narrator The mean old thorny weeds killed every seed that tried to grow with them.

Poor Super Seed thought he'd never get to grow.

Farmer throws more balloons up as he walks to Good Soil at front stage.

Narrator He watched the seeds blow in the wind all day long. He knew that if he didn't try to land soon, he'd die too. He decided to try it at the next breeze.

Farmer goes to Good Soil, waking her up. He throws some balloons on her and kneels down beside her. He rolls some balloons on her belly tickling her.

Narrator The wind came and carried Super Seed and many others to the Good Soil just beyond the weeds.

Farmer takes Super Seed off his shoulder and rolls him into Good Soil's belly.

Narrator The soil felt soft and warm. They all went to sleep inside the quiet blanket of dirt. They slept and got plenty of rain water at night. The sun woke them up for many great mornings.

Farmer backs up on his knees and watches. Good Soil takes Super Seed under her blanket and raises the tree branch.

Narrator Super Seed felt different. He wasn't scared anymore. He felt himself getting bigger and bigger. He noticed the sun coming closer and closer. Slowly all the seeds stretched toward the sky. They sent their roots deep into the good soil and the earth gave them all they ever needed. They grew so big and tall that soon, at the top, *these* seeds saw that they were now plants. And Super Seed saw that he had grown more seeds on top of himself; hundreds of seeds that would some day catch the breeze and fly in the wind as he did. Super Seed sang to the day and shook the top of his branches in happiness.

Farmer raises his arms to the tree branch in thanksgiving as Good Soil shakes the branch.

Narrator He was very happy he took the chance and landed on the Good Soil.

In *Super Seed,* written for clown mimes, the Farmer plants seed in Good Soil.

The Devil and Mr. J.

A play for mimes adapted from Matthew 4:1-11; Jesus' temptation in the desert after his baptism. Lent.

Themes
Sin, grace, baptism, temptation, new life, and strength

Rehearsal Requirement
Two hours on one day prior to Mass and one-half hour just prior to Mass to calm the "jitters." Eighth-grade level mimes are best for the play.

Characters
The Devil (Satan character dressed as a mime with a red oval face outlined in black. He should have clown-white rings around his eyes. See Appendix, Quick Make-up. Pin four red streamers to each arm long enough to touch the floor when his arms are outstretched. Cover everything with a black cape and hood, and wear red or black gloves.)

Mr. J. (Jesus character dressed as a regular mime. He wears a white alb.)

Narrator 1—(adult voice)

Props
3 chairs
Portable Cassette Recorder/Player
Tape of thunder and wind (such as from the records, *Walt Disney's Night on Bald Mountain,* or "Cloudburst" from *Grand Canyon Suite*)

Jesus enters from right stage and walks to front stage and goes down to the floor in a deep bow with his back to the audience.

Narrator
One day there came a tall, thin man to the river Jordan. Everyone there was being baptized. But this man seemed to be a special somebody.

Jesus rises up slowly with his arms to heaven.

Narrator
He was the Son of God, Jesus of Nazareth. He went down into the waters and when He rose up he wasn't quite the same.

Jesus walks around until he comes to the front of the pulpit at left stage. He faces the audience, kneels, and prays while looking toward heaven.

Narrator
Jesus couldn't help but think of his cousin, John, baptizing him. And he wondered about the voice that called him "my Son." He needed somewhere to be alone to think and pray. He found a small desert place out of sight and prayed:

Jesus
Oh God, much has happened today. What does it all mean? Help me to understand what I am to do now.

Jesus bows to the floor level.

Narrator	Jesus stayed in this desert place for forty days and forty nights. He ate no food; just thought about his baptism, and prayed. Many, many times in his prayers he asked for God's help.
Jesus	Oh God, please send me your help here on earth. If I am the Son of God, I need your help.
	Devil enters from right stage and goes to Jesus. His face is covered by the hood. Jesus rises to greet him.
Narrator	Just then a hooded man came into the desert and saw Jesus. He went over to him and said:
	Devil holds out one hand to Jesus.
Satan	Good day, young man. I couldn't help but hear you say that you are Jesus, the Son of God. If you are the Son of God, you must eat.
	The devil takes Jesus to front stage.
Narrator	The hooded man took Jesus to a place near the mountains. He looked all around for a bite to eat.
	Devil points to the floor as Jesus looks around at the stones.
Satan	I'm sorry. There's no food here at all. But, if you are the Son of God, you can turn these stones into bread. Then we can both eat. Surely you can do a miracle; you are God's Son?
	Jesus bends, picks up a stone, and throws it.
Narrator	Jesus was as hungry as one man could be. The stones began to look like bread to his hungry eyes. And he felt as if he "could" do a miracle. But suddenly, he threw the stones as far as he could and said to the hooded man:
	Jesus then turns to the devil and points his finger at his face.
Jesus	Not on bread alone are people to live, but on the Word of God.
	The devil cramps up in laughter.
Narrator	Well, the hooded man laughed as hard as he could:
	The devil holds one hand toward Jesus.
Satan	So you're the Son of God, Jesus of Nazareth. If you can't even feed yourself, you must be a fake. I'll not call you Son of God. I'll call you a man's name, just a man's name—Mr. J. You're not a god; you're just a man. You're just Mr. J.
	The devil takes Jesus to stand upon the chair in the pulpit. The devil stays outside the pulpit with one hand extended to Jesus and the other hand extended toward the floor.
Narrator	The hooded man was very mean to hungry Jesus. And he didn't allow him a minute to pray. He grabbed his arm and took him to the tallest church steeple in the town. Jesus was tired but he went up to the top of the tower with the hooded man. The hooded man spoke:
Satan	I'll give you another chance, Mr. J. Maybe this time you'll prove to me that you are the Son of God. Then I'll call you Jesus, the Son of God. Throw yourself down from this high tower. The Bible tells us that God will send his

	angels to help his Son.
Narrator	But Jesus only said:
	Jesus extends one hand to the devil.
Jesus	You shall not put the Lord your God to the test. I *am* Jesus, the Son of God.
Narrator	The hooded man became very angry and began to shout:
	Devil raises both hands to sky and grabs his head.
Satan	You're not the Son of God. That proves it. You're just Mr. J., a mere man. You can't do miracles.
	The devil leaves Jesus to rock back and forth until he reaches front stage.
Narrator	The hooded man rocked back and forth as if his whole body was changing into something else. He shouted some strange magic words into the sky.
	Play tape of thunder and wind. Stage lights go on and off constantly. The devil goes down to the floor where he flings off his cape and rises up flowing back and forth allowing his streamers to fly out.
Narrator	(Loudly, over the tape) Just then the sky grew black and lightning and thunder cracked. A storm came up in an instant. The wind blew the sand all over. The clouds darkened the desert as if it was nighttime. The lightning struck down to the earth like arrows. Then the wind blew up a twister around the hooded man. His cloak and hood flew off in the wind and he rose up. He took on the shape of the devil. He reached into the storm and waved his arms fiercely. He shouted magic words and the wind came to a stop.
	Abruptly stop the tape just before the word, ''Stop,'' so it will vibrate loudly in the church. The lights are now off.
Narrator	When the storm cleared the devil had Jesus high on a mountaintop.
	The devil runs to Jesus and takes him to stand upon the back stage wall chair. The devil stands on a chair too. Lights on. The devil extends one hand to Jesus, and the other to the floor below.
Satan	Just look at all the cities and towns. And all full of millions of people. Well, Mr. J., I want to believe you are the Son of God. I really don't like calling you Mr. J. I'll tell you what, bow down and worship me and I'll make you King over the whole world. I'll give all this to you and you'll be called King Jesus.
	Jesus turns to the devil and points into his face.
Narrator	Jesus looked into the devil's eye and shouted:
Jesus	You shall worship the Lord your God only, him alone shall you adore. God owns the world and only he can give it away.
Narrator	The devil gave up.
	The devil jumps down from the chair and exits at left stage.
Narrator	He jumped down from the mountaintop and shouted as he left:
Satan	You're just a man, Mr. J.; you're not worth my time.
	Jesus steps down from the chair and slowly exits to right stage looking

toward heaven.

Narrator God was very pleased with his Son Jesus. He didn't give in to the devil's requests. So he sent his angels with jars of cool water, baskets of warm food, and armfuls of his love. They took care of Jesus until he left the desert.

Special Note

1 Two to four months before a children's liturgy takes place, ask if there are any parishioners who would agree to have their infant baptized at a children's liturgy, so that the parish children could better understand what the ceremony means.

2 The homily should be the infant baptism rite. Prepare posters of the symbols so they can be shown to the children; water, candle, oil, and a white robe. Have the children sit around the baptism party as the baptism happens. The homilist should use the posters as these symbols occur in the rite.

3 A good handout (see Appendix, Handouts) is an 8½" x 11" sheet with several lit candles drawn on it side by side. Merely roll them up, candles facing outside, and tape it. Reserve the symbol of the candle for last. When the godparent is asked to light the candle from the Paschal Candle, ask the children to raise their "candles" high. Then proceed with the blessing and explanation. Do not give the children their candles until just before this part of the rite occurs; they'll only fidget and play with them.

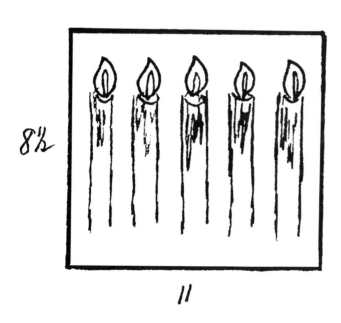

The Wasteful Son

A play for puppets with audience-finger-puppet participation adapted from Luke 15:11 – 32; the prodigal son. Lent.

Themes	Forgiveness, sin, repentance, coming home, and reconciliation
Rehearsal Requirement	Two hours
Characters	Father Older (Older Son) Younger (Younger Son) Motel Owner Friend 1 Friend 2 Narrator (To introduce the play only) Pigs (Audience, with finger puppets)
Props	See Appendix, ''Puppet Stage Construction.'' Cassette Tape Recorder/Player Tape of a door slamming and telephone dialing and ringing.

PUPPET STAGE WITH SCENERY

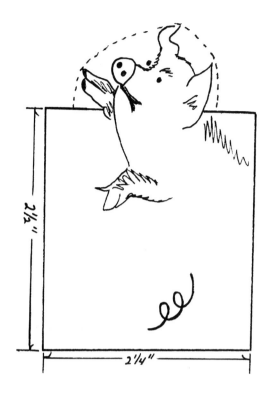

Pig Finger-Puppets Directions

1   Reproduce the above drawings to exact measurements on a ditto or stencil spirit master.

2   Run off the number needed and cut along the outside line and dotted line.

3   Wrap the rectangle around your little finger and tape it closed.

4   If your numbers are small, or if you have plenty of help, add a curly pipe cleaner tail under the tape. You can also glue a cotton ball behind the head.

The audience is seated in front of the puppet stage. They all have pig finger-puppets.

Narrator   Jesus sat down with tax collectors and sinners. All the head priests began to talk about this: "This man welcomes sinners and sits and eats with them." Jesus heard them and said, "Don't you know that the angels sing more over one sinner who comes back to the Father than over all of you so-called church goodies put together?" Then he told everyone this story: "A man had two sons. . . ."

Father, Older, and Younger pop up at left stage above Home.

Father   My two sons, have you both bought new clothes again?

Older	I didn't, Father. But my brother, Younger, did. He's always spending his spend money as soon as he gets it.
Younger	Hey, Older, my brother, just because you're older than me doesn't mean you can talk about me. While we're on the subject, Father, I need more spend money than I get. Older doesn't need so much, but I do.
Older	Wait just a minute . . .
	They begin to argue.
Father	My sons, my sons, stop fighting. We've been blessed with fine clothes, a wonderful home, and all we need to eat. We are even able to pay workers to tend our pigs for us. We are very lucky, Younger. So why do you want more?
	Older leaves. He has no further part.
Older	I'm leaving. I've heard you two talk money too many times before. Good-bye.
Younger	I'm tired of staying around here and always being treated like the younger son. I'm 18 now, and I want to move out on my own. I want to go out and see the world; live my own life—by myself.
Father	But my son, I've given you all you need. And I do love you very much.
Younger	Father, I want out! I know a faraway land where I can make a fresh start. You once said that you were saving some money in the bank for Older and me.
Father	Well, yes I have. As a matter of fact, I have it here in the house safe. It's for your future.
Younger	I want mine now. Older can take care of the pigs for me. He can even have my spend money for doing it. I want my share now.
Father	I know you have become tired of living here. Okay, I'll get your share of the inheritance.
	He goes behind stage and comes up holding the money bag. He gives it to younger.
Father	Here, my son. Take it if you must go.
Younger	All right! Thanks, Father, I'm leaving right now. My bags have been packed and they're inside the workers' house. See ya. Say so long to Older for me.
	Play tape of a door slamming as Father drops behind stage and Younger moves toward the center of the stage.
Younger	(With vigor) Goodbye, workers. And just look at all those pigs. Hold up your finger puppets, children. Hold them high. Oh, how I hated taking care of all those pigs. Just look at them all. Just listen to them. Say "oink, oink" children. Come on, say, "oink, oink." Wow, they are noisier than I thought. Okay, children, quiet. And put your puppets down. It's great to be on my own. A bag of money and no more pigs to look after.
Younger	Just look at all the sights in these different lands. Look at this city. Just look at all the people; and not a pigpen in sight. And look, movies, games, food. Boy, I'm glad I left home. This is the life!

	Now, let's find a place to live. There, over there, there's a motel. That looks like a great place to live.
	He moves over to right side of stage above "Motel." Motel Owner pops up.
Motel Owner	My, that's a big bag of money. Can I help you, sir?
Younger	Yes. My name is Younger and I want to live here, Mr. Motel Owner. I have lots of money . . .
	Friends 1 and 2 pop up.
Younger	. . . lots of money to spend.
Friend 1	Well, I couldn't help but hear a friendly voice. Sure you can live here, and I'll be your friend.
Younger	Who are you guys?
Friend 2	We are now your friends. Here, let me put your money bag over here.
	He takes it and drops it behind stage.
Younger	Gee, this place is sure friendly.
Motel Owner	Hey, I need some money to pay for your room.
Younger	Sure, just take what you need out of the money bag.
	He bends to take money.
Younger	Okay, friends, let's have some fun. I have money, and I want to live the good life. Let's spend, spend, and spend.
Friend 1	Wait, I need my motel bill paid if I'm to stay here another day.
Younger	Just take it out of my money bag. Mr. Motel Owner, take his rent out of my bag.
	Motel Owner bends and gets more money.
Younger	After all, what are friends for? Now, let's go for some fun.
	They head to center of stage.
Younger	Friends, let's take lots of money and go down into the city. All we have to do is spend, and buy, and spend. Let's have a ball. Come on.
	All three bounce around, running left, right, up, down and all around. They ad lib screams, yells, having fun, buying, spending, etc. The dialogue should be frantic, fast moving and loud.
Friend 2	Hey, it's getting late.
Friend 1	Yea, you're right. We'd better be heading back to the motel for some sleep.
Younger	Okay, we'll come back tomorrow again.
	They go to right stage over "Motel." Friends yawn and drop behind stage. Younger sleeps atop stage; snoring to cause laughter. A cock crows.
Younger	(Startled) What, what was that? Oh, it's morning. (Looking down) Oh no, my money! Here's the bag, but it's empty.
	Motel Owner and friends pop up.

Motel Owner	Time to pay for the next day.
	He bends to get money and rises quickly.
Motel Owner	What's this? Your money bag is empty. Is this a joke?
Younger	I don't know how I could have spent it all. Friends, how about lending me some money? I'll pay you back as soon as I can get a job.
Friend 1	Is your money really all gone?
Friend 2	Well, don't expect us to help you.
Younger	But I spent my money on you. Surely, you can help me.
Friend 1 & 2	Sorry, pal. We don't want *poor* friends. We have to go now. Bye.
	They drop behind stage.
Motel Owner	Well, fellow, I need some money if you're going to live here. It's not free you know.
Younger	But I have none. And I'm too far from home to go back now. I'll pay you when I get a job, honest.
Motel Owner	There's a great famine in this land now. Many people are starving and there's no jobs to be had by anyone.
Younger	Oh, only if I hadn't left home. I can't go back now or they'll see how foolish I've been.
Motel Owner	Tell you what. I have three pig pens out back that need cleaning up. I need someone to take care of my pigs, too.
Younger	Oh no, pigs.
Motel Owner	What?
Younger	Nothing. I'll take it.
Motel Owner	You can live out there in the shack next to the pigpens. (Gets two corn husks.) Here, here's their food. They love corn husks. Go ahead, get out. You can't stay in here.
	Motel Owner drops behind stage.
Younger	(Throwing husks to pigs) Hi, pigs. (Somberly) Hi again. You hear me? Raise your puppets, children, raise them high now. Hi, pigs. Here's your crumby food; catch. I hate pigs. Oh, how I hate pigs. But I've got to earn some money to at least have a place to sleep. I'm so hungry I could jump down there and eat with the pigs. What am I going to do? I know it's not your fault, pigs. Go to sleep now. Put your puppets down now, children. Good night piggies. Put them down.
Younger	What am I going to do? What a mess I'm in. My Father's savings are wasted away. I'm trapped without a friend in the world. How stupid I've been. And now I'm all alone. I don't have a paying job. I'll be stuck here till I waste away. My whole life I'll be feeding and sleeping with pigs. I'll never have a friend again. Maybe I could. . . . No, they won't take me back. I hurt my Father too much for him to let me come back home. But maybe. . . . Hey, you kids out there, do you think I could go back home? Huh, what do you think. I can't hear you. Do you think I could go back home?

Waits for response.

Maybe you're right. Even back home my Father's workers have it better than I do right now. Even the workers get regular food to eat; I'm starving here.

Jumps up

Hey, wait a minute, a dime, I found a dime. I'll call home and see if I'm welcome back. Maybe I'd better not. What do you think, kids? Should I call home?

Waits for response.

Tell you what, I'll call and say, "Father, I have sinned against heaven and in your sight. I am sorry for what I have done. I spent all the money you saved for me and I don't deserve to be called your son. Please let me be just one of your workers." You think he'll talk to me, kids?

Waits for response.

Okay, I'll do it. Here's a telephone.

Picks up telephone and play tape of dialing and ringing.

Hello, Father, I have . . . But . . . What! . . . But . . . Okay.

Puts telephone behind stage.

He said, "Come on home, my son. Come home. Come on home."

Father pops up at left stage as Younger runs to him.

Younger   I'm going home! Hello, Father. I have sinned and I am sorry. And I'm glad to be home even if it's to be only a worker.

Father   Oh no, my son. Come, we will have a party for your homecoming. I'll put the best clothes in the house on you. I'll put the best ring I have on your finger. We'll have the biggest party ever.

Younger   Father, I don't understand.

Father   My son was dead and is alive again. He was lost and is now found. Let us celebrate!

Younger   Thanks, Father. You go and I'll be right along. I want to just look around one more time.

They embrace and Father drops behind stage.

Younger   Hello, home! Hello, workers! And hello, pigs! Raise your puppets up, children. Raise them high. Hello all you great big beautiful piggies. I just love you all. I'm home now and I'm going to feed you the very best from now on. Let me hear your "oink, oink." Come on children, let me hear your "oink, oink." Beautiful, just a beautiful sound. It's great to be home again. Goodbye all you beautiful piggies. Goodbye children, and thanks for helping me.

Younger drops behind stage.

Special Note

I   We used the puppet stage as our altar for the Liturgy of the Eucharist. We merely moved the altar table behind the stage and up as close to the front as possible: it made for a beautiful banner.

2   During the Presentation of Gifts we brought the bread, wine, water, and collection down while wearing our puppets. The celebrant bowed and accepted them from the puppets. He even shook their hands and patted them on the head. Then he removed them from our hands and placed them around the top of the stage, leaning over.

Satan addresses Jesus in the play for mimes, *The Devil and Mr. J.,* adapted from Matthew 4:1-11.

One Little Grain of Wheat

A play for costumed players adapted from John 12:24; unless a grain falls and dies. Lent .

Themes   New life, resurrection, Eucharist, trust, faith, and change

Rehearsal Requirement   Two hours one day prior to the Mass. A brief brush-up session a few minutes before Mass is advisable if you choose to use very young children in the play.

Characters   A grain of wheat (Dress: boy—yellow shirt with brown trousers, or girl—yellow dress or blouse with brown skirt or slacks and yellow knee-hi's.)
6 People (Dress: as in the time of Jesus)
Jesus (White alb)
Narrator (Adult)

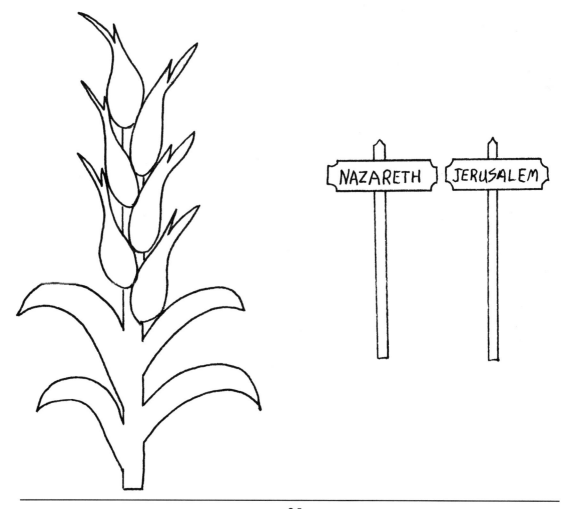

Props   One blossoming wheat stalk made of cardboard or posterboard. The stem and leaves are separate from the wheat grains. The stem is brown and the leaves are green. The grains are yellow and attached to the stem with two-sided tape, which will be removed at the end of the play. Make it at least 3½ feet tall.
A Nazareth and a Jerusalem signpost.
One stick (from the woods) that is at least 3 inches in diameter and 6 feet long.
One large brown blanket (the soil).
Six loaves of Italian bread.

The blossoming wheat stalk is lying on the floor at front stage with the brown blanket. The six loaves of bread are on the floor at left stage. The sign posts are leaning and attached to each side of the altar. The stick is leaning against the center front of the altar: it should extend out approximately 4 feet.

Narrator   Long, long ago there was one little grain of wheat.

Enter wheat grain. She goes to the stick leaning against the altar. Here she embraces it very obviously and freezes attached to it.

Narrator   This little grain of wheat grew on a stalk somewhere between Nazareth and Jerusalem nearly 2000 years ago. This was the land where Jesus lived. And on this same sunny day Jesus was coming by.

Jesus enters walking slowly and thinking.

Narrator   He had been followed by many people all day long. They loved to listen to his words. He taught them many great things.

Enter 6 people behind Jesus. Jesus leads them to the grain of wheat.

Narrator   Jesus paused for a moment next to the wheat stalk; it was a hot afternoon and his feet were aching after walking all morning. Everything he saw on his way was so beautiful to him that he often stopped and talked to the people about the beauty of God's works here on earth. As he rested he noticed the one little grain of wheat clinging to its stalk.

People sit. Jesus takes the grain by her shoulders. He puts her next to him as he removes her from the stalk. The grain's arms are close by her sides; not moving or looking up.

Narrator   He picked the little grain of wheat off its stalk and looked at it.

Narrator   He then held it up to show the people. As he began to talk about it the people moved even closer to him.

People move in around Jesus, who holds out one hand speaking.

Narrator   In a gentle voice, Jesus said, "Just look at this one little grain of wheat. How often we walk right by without seeing the beauty and wonderful story it has to tell. If this grain of wheat does not fall to the ground and die, it will only

26

be a grain of wheat and nothing else. But if it does fall, if it does die, fantastic things will come from it.''

Then Jesus dropped the one little grain of wheat to the ground, and he walked on again.

Jesus places the wheat grain next to the brown blanket at front stage. She gets under the blanket in a crawling position and freezes.

Narrator   The people, now rested too, followed Jesus.

People get up and follow Jesus. They walk next to the wheat grain pretending to step on her.

Narrator   As they all left, they forgot about the one little grain of wheat. Some of them even walked on it grinding it deep into the ground. And there the one little grain of wheat died.

Jesus leads people to right stage where they exit. The people should make their way to the left side of back stage.

Narrator   The one little grain of wheat lay still in the good earth for several days; it was even rained on for two days straight. Then, magically, beneath the ground, something began to happen.

Wheat grain should wiggle beneath the blanket.

Narrator   Little roots began to grow from the grain of wheat. And then a tiny little green shoot appeared just above the ground.

The wheat grain lifts the blanket and grabs the blossoming wheat stalk and raises it upright, slowly.

Narrator   The sun smiled on it so much that it began to grow higher and higher; it tried to touch the warm yellow sun. And then, just as Jesus had said, fantastic things came from the one little grain of wheat. Its stem grew big and strong with long green leaves. And, at the top, it blossomed into hundreds of wheat grains, just as it used to, but even more beautiful.

Wheat stalk is waved back and forth gently as if in the wind.

Narrator   The wheat sang in the gentle breeze, (to the tune of *Mary Had A Little Lamb*)
"Oh, this life is very nice,
Very nice, very nice.
Oh, this life is beautiful,
I'm glad I fell to the ground.''
Then the wheat heard some voices.

Enter people from left stage. They circle around the wheat stalk as if harvesting.

Narrator   They were getting louder and louder. It was the people who worked in the field; they were the same people who followed Jesus when he walked through their town. They were harvesting now. They picked some of the new grains of wheat and went to their home.

People pluck off the wheat grains from the stalk and go to left stage. They lay them down next to the six loaves of bread and pretend to be making bread from wheat grains.

Narrator   They were happy as they got home, for the harvest was plentiful. Many grains of wheat had grown this year. In their kitchens they ground the grains of wheat and made their favorite food—bread.

People, during the above narration, rise up carrying one loaf of bread each! They go to the stripped stalk, hold their loaves high above their heads and circle around the stalk. They bow to the wheat stalk and place their loaves upon the altar. As they are circling the stalk, and once the narration has ended, the Folk Group leads everyone in singing an Alleluia.

Special Note

1   This is a great liturgy to end with a Bread Festival. Announce to the children before Mass and after the final blessing, that they are invited to a party, a Bread Festival. Set up a room nearby with napkins, cups, juice (grape is best) and several whole loaves of Italian Bread.

2   The six loaves can be set in front of the altar on a small table as a banner. Decorate the bottom of the table with the removed grains of wheat from the stalk. During the dismissal have the children actors carry out the bread to the festival room. Once there, the celebrant can bless the food and tell the children to break bread as Jesus did.

3   We advertised three weeks before this liturgy for a family who was willing to bake communion bread for the Mass. We did get a family, and the celebrant mentioned this just before the Communion Rite to enhance the meaning and understanding of the gospel play.

What a Week for Jesus

A play for mimes adapted from Matthew 21:1 – 11, 27:11 – 61; triumphant entry into Jerusalem, and the passion.

Rehearsal Requirement
A three-hour session at least three days prior to the Mass. Another one-hour brush-up rehearsal is good the day or morning before Mass.

Characters
Narrator—(adult)
Jesus—Wearing a white T-shirt with ''Jesus, The King'' on it in black letters, he has a thick bead of red make-up above his eye brows at the hair line (out of immediate sight of the audience).
Pilate—He also plays crowd and soldier. (See Special Note for make-up).
Barabbas—He also plays crowd and soldier.
Simon—He also plays crowd and soldier.
Chief Priest—He also plays crowd and soldier.
Elder—He also plays crowd and soldier.
1 Crowd Person
2 Soldiers
Folk Group—Or several people planted in a side pew with the audience. No special dress is required for them—just a loud speaking part.

Props
Several palms
Large wooden cross (approximately 6' high and 1½'' thick)
Red robe
Stick (three feet long)
Hammer (the larger, the better)

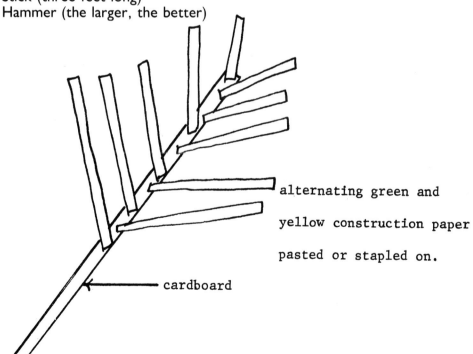

alternating green and yellow construction paper pasted or stapled on.

cardboard

Stick with a sponge tied to one end (five feet long)
Cassette recorder/player
Tape of "Hosanna" (side two, last three stanzas, 1½ minutes) and "John Nineteen Forty One" (side 4, 2 minutes) from the album *Jesus Christ, Superstar,* "Dear Father" (side 4, 75 seconds) from the album *Jonathan Livingston Seagull,* and "Finale" (side 2, third stanza only, 1 minute) from *Godspell.* (Other fitting music can be used in place of these suggestions.)
"Jerusalem" placard (black letters)
"Jesus, King of the Jews" placard (red letters) with nail.
Paper towel

Staging   Letters on the stage drawing correspond to lettered props and their placement before the opening of the mime.

Props are placed on the stage as "Staging" indicates. Jesus is at the back of the center aisle. Other mimes are backstage—four to the left and four to the right. They are holding several palm branches in their hands.

Narrator   What a week for Jesus it was to be. "Today's the day!" the people of Jerusalem shouted. Jesus, the great prophet, the Messiah, the long awaited king of the Jews was coming to the city. He would spend only one week there, his last week on earth. The people wanted to give their king a parade. They ripped branches off the palm trees and ran out to the city gates to see their king, Jesus. The chief priest and elders didn't like all the people paying so much attention to this Jesus. But the people didn't listen to them. They only ran out singing: "Hosanna to the Son of David! Blessed is he who comes in the name of the Lord! Hosanna in the highest!"

Into the microphone play the tape of "Hosanna" from *Jesus Christ Superstar.* Mimes enter at right and left stages waving palms and greeting those seated up front. They shake hands with the people, pat kids on the head, smile at everyone, give out some palms until they meet at front stage with Jesus. Jesus enters down the center aisle slowly. He holds his arms out greeting the people as the King of Glory. As the song comes to an end they all meet at front stage. Jesus faces the audience as mimes face him while kneeling and waving their palms. Jesus continues outstretching his arms to the audience. When the song ends, Jesus and mimes go to Center Stage and "mill around" in a circle. Their heads and arms are down as narration continues.

Narrator   Jesus wasn't in the city long before the chief priests and elders knew they had to find a way to get rid of him. You see, they were in charge of the church in Jerusalem and people were looking to Jesus as king of their church. They felt that Jesus was after their job. So they planned to take him to court by getting their friends to tell lies about him. They would say that he broke their laws.

Mimes break into a courtroom scene at center stage. Pilate stands in the center facing Jesus. His arms are folded until he speaks to Jesus, at which time he points into his face. The Chief Priest and Elder hold Jesus by his arms to the side of Pilate so the audience can see him. One mime lines up behind Jesus. The four others line up on the other side of Pilate. Some mimes should go down on one knee as they observe.

Narrator   The chief priest and elder brought Jesus before Pilate. Pilate was the judge of the whole land in Jerusalem. Many people came and told lies about Jesus. But Jesus didn't answer them. Jesus knew he was innocent. Pilate asked Jesus, "Don't you hear what they are saying about you?" Jesus remained silent. Pilate continued, "Are you the king of the Jews?" Jesus looked at Pilate and said, "As you say." Pilate knew that Jesus wasn't guilty.

Pilate grabs Barabbas and Jesus, and pulls them next to him. Mimes back off a bit and all go down on one knee.

Narrator   Pilate figured that the Priests and Elders were just jealous of Jesus and wanted to teach him a lesson. "They probably wanted him to leave the city," he thought. So he remembered that it was a festival week. They had an old custom that allowed the judge to free one prisoner if the people approved it. Pilate thought, "I'll grab the worst, meanest prisoner in jail. I'll offer the people Jesus or the bad prisoner. Surely they'll take Jesus."

Narrator   Pilate grabbed Barabbas, the meanest criminal in jail. He even killed people. "Because it's festival week," Pilate said to the crowd, "I am releasing one prisoner to you. Today, you have a choice, Jesus or Barabbas." Pilate just knew they would let Jesus go free. He said, "Which one do you want me to set free?"

Folk group yells, "Barabbas! Give us Barabbas!" Mimes raise fists as they too indicate the same. Pilate, confused, raises arms to crowd.

Narrator   Pilate was surprised. He asked the crowd, "Then what am I to do with Jesus, the so-called king of the Jews?"

Folk group yells, "Nail him to the cross. Crucify him." Mimes do same with fists.

Narrator   Pilate knew that crucifixion would mean death to Jesus. And he didn't do anything wrong for such an awful way to die. Pilate shouted back, "Why, what crime did Jesus commit?"

Folk group chants, "Crucify him, crucify him, crucify him!" Mimes use fists again.

Narrator   Pilate couldn't get a straight answer out of the crowd. He was afraid they'd break out into a riot so he called for a bowl of water.

One mime bends to pick up an imaginary bowl of water for Pilate.

He dipped his hands into the bowl and said, "Okay, but I wash my hands of this whole matter. It is you, you people out there, you are sending this Jesus to the cross—not me."

Pilate washes his hands and shakes them dry. He points and accuses the audience.

Folk group yells, "Crucify him. Give us Barabbas and crucify Jesus. We'll be to blame, us and our children." Mimes use fists one last time. Pilate pushes Barabbas into the crowd of mimes. All mimes now become soldiers and take Jesus, roughly, to right stage.

Narrator   Pilate released Barabbas to the crowd. He had his soldiers take Jesus to their jail until they had time to get his cross ready.

Soldiers mime stripping Jesus, place red robe about his shoulders and place the 3' stick in his hand.

Narrator   The soldiers ripped the clothes off Jesus. They all laughed at him and took turns hitting him. One soldier got the bright idea to dress Jesus up to look like the king of the Jews. They placed an old robe about his shoulders and laughed. One soldier found a stick and placed it in his hand as a king's ruling scepter. Jesus just hung his head down. He was very sad.

One soldier goes toward front stage looking and finding thorns. He places a crown upon Jesus' head while placing 4 fingers over Jesus' thick bead of red make-up at his hair line. He pulls his fingers down over the red line and down to Jesus' eyebrows—to symbolize bleeding wounds. He reaches down to the floor and inconspicuously wipes his fingers with the paper towel.

Narrator   Then another soldier looked around for a king's crown. He saw some sticker bushes nearby and pulled a few strands out. He rolled them up into a crown and stuck it on Jesus' head. He pushed it down hard until the thorns went into his skin and he began to bleed. They all laughed very hard.

All soldiers bow down to their knees, laughing. Jesus stands with head down.

Narrator   They even bowed down on their knees laughing at this funny looking king. They said, "All hail the king, the king of the Jews."

They rise, remove robe and let it drop to the floor. They take the stick and hit him once, and let it fall to the floor. They raise up the cross and place it upon his shoulders. Jesus carries it on his left shoulder so his body and face are facing the audience. Soldiers point to left stage.

Narrator   When they were tired of making a fool of Jesus they got up. One soldier took the robe off Jesus. Another quickly grabbed the stick out of his hand and he beat him again. They all laughed again. The soldiers put Jesus' clothes back on him and took him out of the jail. They gave him his cross to carry all the way to the top of the hill called, Golgotha. Jesus was so beaten up and tired he couldn't believe that they wanted him to carry that heavy mean looking cross. "To the top, king of the Jews," one soldier shouted as they all pointed to Golgotha.

Two soldiers kick Jesus as he begins to walk around the outer limits of the staging area.

Narrator They kicked him as he started the long climb.

Soldiers line up behind Jesus as he walks from right stage to front to left stage. He falls three times; the third at left stage. Play tape of "Dear Father" from *Jonathan Livingston Seagull* as Jesus walks.

Narrator When Jesus fell for the third time, the soldiers were afraid he would die before they got to the top. So they picked a strong man in the crowd. His name was Simon. They forced him to carry the cross for Jesus.

Soldiers grab Simon and force him to carry the cross to center stage. He then lays it down so Jesus can lie upon it in full view of the audience.

And Simon did it; he was too scared of all the soldiers to say no. Besides, he felt sorry for Jesus. He looked into Jesus' eyes and carried his cross to the top of the hill.

Soldiers lay Jesus upon the cross. Jesus stretches his hands out upon the cross. One soldier takes the hammer and pounds three times at each hand. He should hit the cross loudly. All soldiers now go down to one knee evenly distributed at the top and bottom of the cross. Soldier closest to Jesus' head nails the "Jesus, King of The Jews" placard to the cross.

Narrator When they reached the top of Golgotha the soldiers laid Jesus upon the cross. Jesus couldn't believe his eyes when he saw a soldier get out long nails and a hammer. But he was too tired to pull away. The soldier hammered a nail into Jesus' right hand (pause for hammering). Then he nailed his other hand into the splintered wood of the cross (pause for hammering). Another soldier nailed a sign to the top of the cross and laughed.

Jesus, in a crouched position, rolls toward back stage and remains still. Soldiers raise the cross. Simon holds it from behind as Jesus is placed before it. Jesus grabs the top cross piece and holds it. All mimes sit around the foot of the cross.

Narrator They lifted the cross and dropped it into a small hole so it would stand firm. The soldiers sat around waiting for Jesus to die. They even rolled dice for his clothes. They left him with nothing; not even his last piece of clothing.

Jesus rolls his head to and fro. Elder rises and gets the stick with a sponge tied to it. He raises it to Jesus. High Priest raises his hand to stop him. Elder places it down and returns to his place.

Narrator Jesus cried out, "Eli, Eli, lema sabbachthani?" That means, "My God, My God, why have you forsaken me?" This call to God scared the Elder who quickly grabbed a sponge. He dipped it in a bucket of old cheap wine and raised it up on a stick to offer Jesus a drink. But the chief priest stopped him and said, "Wait. He's calling on God to help him. Let's see if God will do it." Once again Jesus cried out and began to give up his spirit.

Play tape of "Finale" from *Godspell*. Jesus should mime with his head and facial expression as the words of the song indicate. He dies by dropping his head to one side.

Narrator There was a terrible wind storm when Jesus died, and the earth trembled.

One soldier rises up to her knees and raises one arm toward Jesus.

Narrator   One soldier even said, "Clearly, this was the Son of God." Some friends took Jesus off the cross and carried him off to their tomb to be buried.

Play tape "John Nineteen Forty One" from *Jesus Christ Superstar*. Mimes take Jesus down from the cross. They lay him before the cross on his back with his hands crossed over his chest. Simon lays the cross against the altar behind him. Mimes line up four to a side of Jesus. They each place their hands under him and, together, raise him up to their shoulders. Jesus remains stiff. All mimes turn facing audience. Jesus lets his head hang back with his eyes closed. They carry Jesus out, slowly, by way of the center aisle, as he came in.

Narrator   (After mimes pass by and while music is still playing) What a week for Jesus it was to be. "Today's the day!" the people of Jerusalem shouted. Jesus, the great prophet, the messiah, the long awaited king of the Jews was coming to the city. He would spend only one week there—only one week. And what a week for Jesus!

Special Note

1   It is a good idea to have your tapes in order or, if possible, have the correct music on one tape.

2   Follow the make-up directions as suggested in the Appendix. Instead of a black tear line through the eyes, give Pilate a black circle around his eyes. All of the soldiers can have several black lines at different angles about the face. The more morbid they appear the better the effect.

3   Once the mime is over and the homily is finished, place the cross on its side in front of the altar as a banner. Place the hammer, palms, and robe around the cross also.

4   For the blessing of the palms, which is normally done at the beginning of Mass just before the Entrance Rite, organize a first grade, or two, to participate. Have them create their own palms made in class several days before the performance. They should sit in the front pews and when the celebrant has blessed the palms, they should follow him in procession waving their palms. The celebrant stops in the back of the church as the children process to the altar. They line both sides of the aisle. As the Entrance Song begins they lay their palms on the floor. The celebrant enters, walking over the palms, wearing the same red robe that the soldiers will use to ridicule Jesus in the jail; he can place it in position after the opening prayer.

The Great Sheep Mix-Up

A play for clowns and mimes adapted from John 10:27 – 30, 14; the Good Shepherd. Easter.

Themes   Naming, belonging, baptism, God's Family, membership, faith, and trust.

Rehearsal Requirement   Two hours one day prior to the Mass and a refresher one-half hour before Mass.

Characters   The Good Shepherd (a clown mime)
Lester Shepherd (a clown mime)
Nester Shepherd (a clown mime)
Nine Sheep (regular mimes)
Narrator (an adult)

Props   9 Sheep's Head Sticks (see drawing below)
1 Shepherd's Staff (see drawing below)

Lester is at the back of the right side aisle with three sheep. Nester is at the back of the left side aisle with three sheep. The Good Shepherd, with his staff, is at the back of the center aisle with three sheep. All of the sheep are carrying a Sheep's Head Stick just above their head holding it close to one side of their face: it should always be held there firmly throughout the play. Lester and Nester begin herding their mischievous sheep toward the center stage. Their sheep stray, bump, turn, stop, etc.; they make it very difficult for their shepherds to keep them together as one flock.

Narrator What a mixed up day for some shepherds and some sheep. There once was two shepherds, Lester and Nester. They were allowed to graze their sheep in the same meadows for years now. The sheep were so used to going the same way every day they could almost get there without a shepherd. Everybody was content—shepherds, and sheep.

But today, a very mixed-up day, Lester and Nester were ordered to take their sheep to different meadows. As a matter of fact, Lester was ordered to Nester's meadow, and Nester to Lester's. No one could make any sense out of it. All of the meadows were still in use, but all the shepherds had to switch around.

Lester and Nester should be very close to the stage area now. Lester is aiming for left stage while Nester is aiming for right.

Narrator Lester was headed for his new meadow to the north. And Nester was herding his sheep to his new meadow to the south. They didn't understand it all but they obeyed.

Lester and Nester are on right and left stage now, respectively. They both try to stop their sheep unsuccessfully. The sheep push them down and mix together at center stage where they walk around close together; they are never still.

Narrator Lester was nearing his meadow when he saw his friend, Nester, heading right for him. "Oh no," he thought, "Our sheep will collide and get all mixed-up."

And Nester noticed his friend's sheep coming toward him. And he tried to stop his sheep too. "Wait, you mangy sheep. Stop, you'll get all mixed-up. Hold on. Wait." But the sheep just went right over them. "You dumb bags of wool! Come back here!" But the sheep ran together and became very mixed-up. You couldn't tell one from the other. They all looked alike.

Lester and Nester get up brushing themselves off while moving closer to center stage. They wave fists at each other.

Narrator Lester got up and blamed Nester for the whole mess. Nester became angry and blamed Lester.

The Good Shepherd starts to walk down the center aisle toward center stage. His sheep follow very orderly in a straight line behind him. Lester and Nester continue arguing while each pulls out, from the mixed-up sheep, one or two sheep. As they fight, the sheep go back into the mix-up.

Narrator As they were yelling at one another, they tried to figure out which sheep belonged to whom. Lester shouted at Nester, "Hey, wait just a minute. You have one of my sheep." Nester shouted back, "And you have taken more sheep than you started with. Give some to me." They came closer, yelling and shouting. Well, push led to shove, and they began to fight.

The Good Shepherd and his flock are at front stage now.

Narrator   Just then they noticed another shepherd coming with a flock of sheep. He was heading for the east meadow and that would lead him right into their sheep mix-up. They run out to try to stop the sheep before things got even more mixed-up. But once again the sheep won; they ran over Lester and Nester. The Good Shepherd calmly watches.

The sheep mix in at center stage.

"Will you just look at that," Nester cried. "Now we'll never be able to separate our sheep. You can't tell them apart now." Lester turned to this new shepherd and said, "Why didn't you try to stop your sheep. Now you'll never get the same sheep back that you started with."

The Good Shepherd answers with his back to the audience and both hands out.

Narrator   The new shepherd replied, "I am the Good Shepherd. I know my sheep, and mine know me." "Oh, sure they do," laughed Nester. Again, Lester and Nester tried to separate the great sheep mix-up. But they still couldn't figure which sheep was theirs. The Good Shepherd was getting a drink from a near-by spring. This made them very angry. "Why aren't you helping us figure out which sheep are ours?" Nester shouted.

The Good Shepherd rises up, still with his back to the audience, and raises his arms to Lester and Nester. At "The Father and I are one" he raises his hands up to heaven, turns and leaves by the center aisle. His sheep, all but one, follow him.

Narrator   The Good Shepherd rose up and said, "My sheep hear my voice. I know them, and they follow me. I give them eternal life, and they shall never perish. No one shall snatch them out of my hand. My Father is greater than all, in what he has given me, and there is no snatching out of his hand. The Father and I are one." With that, he continued on to the East meadow. And his sheep knew his voice, and followed him.

Lester watches the Good Shepherd and his sheep go by him. After the last sheep passes by the one remaining in the mix-up runs out to go with his Good Shepherd. As he runs by Lester he bumps him over again. Lester falls but still watches from the floor. Nester sneaks back to the mix-up and rounds up all the sheep and herds them off at right stage where they exit.

Narrator   Nester saw Lester watching the Good Shepherd and decided to sneak back to the great sheep mix-up and take all of the sheep to his meadow. After all it was beginning to get dark and the sheep hadn't eaten all day.

Lester turns to see what Nester is doing, rises quickly, fumbles around as he chases after him and the flock. He exits after them.

Narrator   Then Lester saw his friend, Nester, stealing all the sheep. He got up quickly and ran after him. You could hear them fighting again as they traveled out of sight just over the next hill. What a mixed-up day for some shepherds and some sheep.

Special Note

I   The Sheep's Head Sticks make an excellent altar banner when they are leaned up and around it.

2   At the closing song, the celebrant might carry one or two of the Sheep's Head Sticks out with him (high up over his head).

3   This reading lends itself very easily to a homily and theme on belonging and naming. How did we get our name? Does our name make us special? When we get lost do people first ask us our name? When we call our pet a different name does it come to us?

4   A good Invitation and Bulletin Insert (see Appendix) is a name tag. Ask the children to put their name on it and wear it to the Mass.

The Good Shepherd, dressed as a clown, gathers his ''sheep,'' mimes holding head sticks.

The Room Upstairs

A play for puppets from Acts 2; Pentecost.

Rehearsal Requirement   Two hours.

Characters   Apostles—
    Peter (also holds and speaks for Apostle 7)
    John (also holds and speaks for Apostle 8)
    Matthew (also holds and speaks for Apostle 9)
    James (also holds and speaks for Apostle 10)
    Thomas (also holds and speaks for Apostle 11)
    Matthias (also holds and speaks for Apostle 12)
Woman's Voice
Old Woman
Beggarman
Folk Group (or a planted adult group in the audience)

Props   Hammer (for sound effects of door knocks and thunder)
Cassette Recorder/Player—portable
Cassette tape of
    1. door slamming
    2. footsteps running upstairs
    3. soft instrumental background music
4' stick with 3 small lit candles tied to the top part.

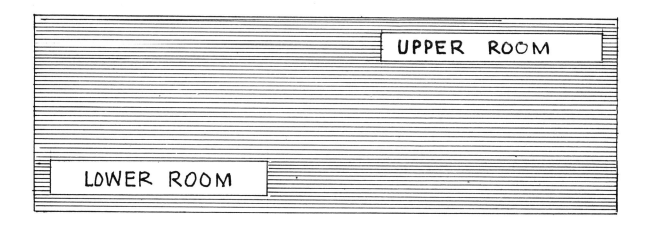

Staging   See Appendix: Puppet Stage Construction

Note   When there is a speaking part for a puppet, it is moved to the very front of the stage. It should be moved so that it is easily understood who is speaking. If arms become tired, or it is difficult to manipulate reading the tacked-up script, or speaking into a microphone with two puppets held up, merely put it down. Raise him back up when it is his turn to speak. Try to keep at least one of your hand puppets up at all times. This whole script can be taped and played as the action begins.

Start tape and play the door slamming and the footsteps running upstairs. Peter, John, and Matthew pop up at "upper room" side of stage. Tape off.

John   Man, you guys, I've never been so scared. Did you see how close I came to being thrown in jail? Matthew, did you see?

Matthew   No, John, I was too busy running to keep up with Peter.

Peter   Well, I just wanted to get here early to straighten up before the other apostles arrive. I wanted to get things in order for our prayer service. Things must be just right. Know what I mean, John?

John   Let's face it, we're all scared. We don't know who we can tell our story to; I want to tell people about our Lord, Jesus, but, if they arrest me, I can't tell anyone. Where did Jesus get his courage? How would he have handled that woman yelling, "Over here, over here, soldiers. Here're some more Christians preaching." I wonder why we ran? I wonder where Jesus got his courage?

Peter   From God. Maybe someday we'll get that same courage. All we can do is keep meeting like this, and praying.

They straighten up the room as three knocks break the silence. All three huddle in fear, as they look to "lower room" side of stage.

Peter   Who, who's there?

Rest of Apostles   It's us, the rest of the twelve apostles. Let us in, quickly! Come on guys! The soldiers may see us!

All apostles pop up at "upper room" side of stage. They embrace in "hello's."

Peter   Come on up. Were you guys followed? Thomas, were you?

Thomas   No. No, but we almost got caught. One woman recognized us as Jesus' followers and ran for the Roman soldiers. Tell them, James.

40

James	We were going to tell our story of Jesus but we were afraid they'd laugh and turn us over to the soldiers. Then . . .
	All begin telling each other stories of close calls. All but Peter.
Peter	Apostles, apostles! Come on guys. Let's begin our prayer service.
	They gather around and bow their heads. Tape of background music on.
Peter	(Raises up) It's been seven weeks now since our Lord, Jesus, died and was raised. Only just two days ago we saw him rise into the sky and disappear into a cloud. We all saw the two men appear to us and say, "Why are you gazing into the sky? Jesus has gone away to heaven, and some day, just as he went, he will return.'' (Bows down)
Apostle 7	(Raises up) Where has our Lord gone? (Bows down)
Apostle 8	(Raises up) Why has he left us alone? (Bows down)
Apostle 9	(Raises up) Why didn't he tell us what to do? (Bows down)
Apostle 10	(Raises up) What can we do? (Bows down)
Apostle 11	(Raises up) What can we do? We are only unarmed apostles. (Bows down)
Apostle 12	(Raises up) We can't tell our story of Jesus with all these soldiers around. (Bows down)
Matthias	(Raises up) And so many people here don't understand our language. And we don't understand theirs. (Bows down)
Peter	(Raises up) You're so right, Matthias. Dear God of Abraham, help us! Our Messiah, Jesus, made promises to us. He said he would never leave us. But now we are alone. What did it all mean? God, give us understanding—if it is your will. Oh, God, you told the prophets of old what to . . .
	Tape off. Three knocks are heard at the door, via the hammer. All huddle in fear again.
John	Oh, no! We've been found out! It's the soldiers I bet! Man, what'll we do now? Is there a back door to this place? Come on, Matthew!
	All talk of how to escape in pandemonium while searching for a rear entrance. Another three knocks pierce the chatter.
Matthew	Wait a minute. Quiet! I'll speak and pretend I'm the only one here. Be cool, apostles, be cool!
	All line up behind him, pushing, as he looks to "lower room" side of stage.
Matthew	Yes? Who is it?
Woman's Voice	It's the landlady. When are you guys going to pay the rent? You're a week overdue now. I can't put food on my table with prayers. And speaking of food; you're not getting any more food up there until your rent's paid up, understand?
Matthew	Yes, woman. You'll get your rent tomorrow. I'll put a check in the mail this afternoon.
Woman's Voice	You'd better. When I get my check in my hot little hands, the food'll be back up to you in the morning. But not a minute before.

Apostles breathe a sign of relief. All bow again. They resume praying. Tape on again.

Peter   (Raises up) See what I mean, God? We're afraid of just a knock at the door. We're afraid of something before we even know what it is. And now, with money running low in our checking account, it looks as if we'll even lose our upper room to pray in. (Bows down)

John   (Raises up) Apostles, let us pray in silence for God to answer us. (Bows)

Tape off. Raise up the four-foot stick with the lit candles tied to the top. Wave it slowly back and forth over the Apostles. Hammer starts pounding slowly and lightly, but increasing until it is hard and furious, simulating thunder. Lower stick and stop hammering. All apostles raise up again.

Peter   Apostles, did you hear?

John   Maybe it was an earthquake or plane crash?

Matthew   Apostles, I felt something funny.

Three knocks are heard again, but no one is fearful.

Peter   Yes? Who is it?

Woman's Voice   It's me again, your landlady. I thought, you were all up there. What's going on up there? Are you guys running around or throwing rocks on the floor? What was that loud noise?

Peter   No, woman. We are only praying before we go out to tell the people of Jesus, our Messiah. His name was, his name *is* Jesus Christ.

All Apostles   Yes, we are only praying before we go out to spread the Good News of Christianity.

Woman's Voice   Oh, okay. If you say so. Boy, you guys used to be so quiet and scared. Now, just listen to all of you! Your tongues are on fire with talk of this Jesus. And you say women talk a lot! Well, keep it down in the upper room; the couple in the lower room is complaining. And don't forget the check!

Peter   Apostles, did you hear? Did you see us? We weren't afraid! We spoke out boldly of Jesus. We even called his story the "Good News." We *did* feel something funny! The Spirit Jesus promised has come into the world—into us!

All Apostles   Yes, now we understand! Our prayer is answered! Praise the Lord: Praise the Lord! Praise the Lord!

John   Matthew, apostles, let's write the whole life of Jesus in a book—a book for everyone to read.

Matthew   Okay, let's do it! We could call it "The Almanac."

John   No. That's no good. Let's call it the "Complete Encyclopedia of Jesus." What do you say, Thomas?

Thomas   No. I've got it! Call it "The Bible." We can all write our own story as we saw it and lived it. We can call them gospels.

All nod in agreement, except Peter.

John	Let's put it at the end of our Scriptures. We can call our Scriptures, up to now, ''The Old Testament.'' And we can call our new books, ''The New Testament.'' What do you think, Peter? You're our leader.
Peter	Well, I'm not much of a writer. But we do understand it all now since we received the Holy Spirit. I think we are so full of God now that we should go out into the world and *tell* the people what we saw. Let's begin building Jesus' Church right now!
John	But, Peter, this book we plan will tell them all about it. We can even have it published in different languages. Come on, Peter, I'll help you write yours. It'll reach all the people, and faster.
Peter	No. The Spirit wants us to move out now—today. I'll tell you what. Later on I'll write you a couple of letters. After ten or twenty years, when you write your Gospels, you can publish my letters with them. By then, we'll all be too old to roam around and we'll have other apostles to go out with the Spirit. Then we can sit back and write. But now, we must spread the Good News in the streets and byways. We are no longer afraid. We now know, as Jesus did, that with God, no one can stop us.
	All nod in agreement.
Matthias	But, Peter, how'll we speak to the Spanish people down the street?
Peter	Matthias, like this: *Como esta usted, mi amigo?*
Matthias	*Muy bien, gracias.* Peter, I did it! I spoke Spanish and I understood you when you spoke it to me. And I've never had a class in Spanish! God is with us and we can do anything! I say, Peter is right. Let's gather our flock starting today. It's all clear now.
	All nod in agreement.
James	Let's test what we have. What do you say, Thomas?
Thomas	Yes, James, you're right. Let's do it now. Let's test it.
All Apostles	Yes, we agree. Look here. Here are all these children. They speak something called ''English.'' None of us have ever studied English. Let's see if they can understand us.
Peter	Okay.
	He turns to the audience. Hang the puppet over the stage as you speak to them.
Peter	My children, can you hear me? (Pause) Can you understand me? (Pause) John, do you hear?
John	Children, see if you understand this? One plus one equals two. Right? (Pause)
	Apostles embrace one another in joy.
All Apostles	They understand! We can speak English, too!
John	Matthew, you try.
Matthew	It's a miracle! Children, is Jesus Christ risen from the dead? (Pause) Did he

die for us? (Pause) Did we receive the Holy Spirit? (Pause) Is God with us even now? (Pause)

Folk Group or planted adult group in the audience, shout, "Aw, they're all drunk! Listen to what they're saying. They're all drunk on wine."

Matthew What's that? Peter, that group in the back there, the adults, they're saying we're all drunk!

Tape on.

Peter (To adults) Listen, all of you visitors and residents of Jerusalem alike! Some of you are saying we are drunk. It isn't true. Besides it's too early for that. No! What you see this morning was predicted centuries ago by the prophet, Joel—"In the last days, God said, I will pour out my Holy Spirit upon all humankind, and your sons and daughters shall prophesy, and your young men shall see visions, and your old men dream dreams. Yes, the Holy Spirit shall come upon all my servants, women and men alike, and they shall prophesy. And I will cause strange demonstrations in the heavens and on the earth." These children know Jesus. They are happier because they now believe. Believe brothers and sisters. Believe and live again, forever! Children, shout out, "Praise God!" (Pause) Shout it louder. (Pause) Apostles, God is with us. His Spirit is in the whole world. These children even have him. Let's all thank God the Father, the Son, and the Holy Spirit, before we go out to preach the Good News.

All bow heads in prayer. Continue tape a few seconds as they are bowed: then, tape off. Old Woman pops up at "lower room" side of stage with hunched Beggarman. They walk to middle stage where all apostles rise and meet them.

Peter Old woman, where are you taking this beggarman?

Old Woman Sir, he has been crippled like this since he was born. I take him out to the main gate of the city every day so he may beg for money to buy food.

Peter Beggarman, (he looks up sideways) we have no money to offer you. Our bank account is low. But I'll give you something else. I command you, in the name of Jesus, Walk!

Beggarman slowly straightens up, shouts, and jumps for joy. All apostles embrace.

Beggarman I saw this Jesus once. I believed in him. But, but, sir, they all say He is dead.

Peter He is risen! He lives! His Spirit is with us now and forevermore!

Old Woman Sir, quiet! Soldiers are only around the corner!

Peter No matter, old woman, they can't hurt us now. We're not afraid anymore.

Beggarman I believe! Praise God! Come, my helper, and let's go to the church to give thanks and tell everyone about this *Good News*.

Exit Beggarman and Woman. Tape on.

Peter Brothers, we have the power of the Holy Spirit. With God we can do anything. We shall never die nor be afraid again. We're not alone. We never were. Now, we're ready to go out into the world. Let's go with God. God is our strength. We were open to his Spirit and he came to us. Now let's allow the Spirit to work through us. We are in God's hands. Come, brothers, let's leave here to say "hello" to life.

Exit all. Fade out tape to off.

Special Note

1   Use the puppet stage as your altar. Merely move it forward and slide your table in behind it. Do all of this as the collection is being taken up just before the Offertory.

2   Have the puppeteers, with their puppets on their hands, bring up the offertory gifts. The celebrant should also remove the puppets from their hands and place them around the top of the altar.

3   At dismissal, the celebrant puts the "Peter" puppet on, removes the "upper room" piece of scenery, and exits holding them high.

4   A good handout is a paper tongue of fire to be colored with a "Spirit" prayer on the back (see Appendix: Handouts).

An example of children's art used in the slide-play, *Jairus' Daughter Is Dead*.

Jairus' Daughter Is Dead

A play of slides created by children adapted from Luke 8:40 – 42, 49 – 56.

Themes	New life, faith, trust, power of Jesus, resurrection, and growth
Rehearsal Requirement	None
Characters	Narrator
Props	35 mm camera (with color slide film) yellow 3' by 3' poster board slide projector movie screen
Staging	None
Preparation	This play involves one entire class of parochial school or CCD children. It is best to begin your preparation at least five weeks before the liturgy. The script for the narration that follows is broken down into numbered verses. Select one to three children for each verse. Give them their verses typed on a sheet of paper and ask them to draw a picture of what it says. They are to draw it on an 8½'' x 11'' piece of white paper using felt-tip pens only (they are brighter for photographing). Make sure they letter their names and grades on their drawings. Pre-number every paper on the back so that you will know which verse a certain drawing pertains to. They can do this at home.

Once all of the drawings are returned to you, arrange them in the correct order. Place the first page in the center of a 3' x 3' yellow poster board on the floor. Stand on a chair and focus your 35-mm camera as close as it allows; the yellow posterboard will show up as a colorful border. Photograph each drawing in this fashion. If you can afford it, take two shots of each picture, just to play it safe.

When you are finished photographing the pages, draw a title picture and one introducing the grade who created these slides. Photograph these two also; these two will be shown first in the program.

After developing the pictures arrange your slides in the slide projector's carousel and preview them while reading the narration. During the actual showing at the Children's Liturgy be prepared to pause several times as parents, grandparents, and kids "ooo and aaah."

All that is left is to show your corresponding slides as you read the verses.

First two slides, title and introduction, are shown without narration.

Narrator

Verse 1 It was a bright sunny day. Jesus was talking to a crowd that had gathered at the bottom of a mountain. He saw a man running down the mountain in a terrible hurry.

Verse 2 It was Jairus, the leader of the local church. He burst through the crowd. He was dressed in beautiful clothes. But that didn't bother Jairus, for he fell down in front of Jesus.

Verse 3 He felt Jesus' hand touch his chin as he raised his sad face. "Jesus," he said, "my little daughter is vey sick at home. Can you come with me at once to heal her?"

Verse 4 Jesus shook his head and said, "Let's go quickly then." And the whole crowd followed them up the mountain. They wanted to see what Jesus would do.

Verse 5 They all rushed down the other side of the mountain and followed the wooded path next to the big sea. They could see Jairus' big yellow house off in the distance.

Verse 6 They were very close to the house when they noticed one of the doctors running out to meet them. He looked at Jairus and said, "Your daughter is dead; do not bother the Teacher, Jesus, any further."

Verse 7 Jesus took Jairus by the arms and said, "Do not be sad and afraid. What you need now is trust. Your little girl's life will be spared."

Verse 8 Jesus and Jairus went into the house. There were many people inside. They were all crying, "Jairus' daughter is dead." Jesus ordered everyone outside. "This is not the house of the dead," he said; "stop crying, she is not dead but asleep."

Verse 9 As they left two doctors stopped in the doorway and said, "We are learned doctors. We examined the little girl and she is surely dead." They laughed at Jesus and left, slamming the door.

Verse 10 Jesus entered the little girl's bedroom with Jairus and his wife. The little girl lay motionless upon her bed. She was not breathing and looked dead. Her mother started to cry again as Jesus went closer to the bed.

Verse 11 Jesus knelt next to the bed and took the little girl's hand. He whispered, "Get up, child." Her mother and father watched from a dark corner. Jesus said again, "Little girl, get up."

Verse 12 The little girl sat up, looked around, and hugged Jesus. She saw her mommy and daddy coming over and said, "I'm hungry." With tears in their eyes they smiled at her.

Verse 13 Jairus flung open the window and showed his little girl to the crowd. He yelled, "She lives, she's alive." Everyone cheered for Jairus, for his wife, for his little girl, and for Jesus. The doctors just turned their back to him and left.

Verse 14 That night they all sat down to a big festive dinner. Jairus put Jesus at his place; the head of the table. And as they ate Jairus' daughter danced for them.

Verse 15   After dinner, Jesus' apostles came for him. As the moon climbed to the top of the mountain, Jesus left. Jairus waved, his wife waved, and their little girl ran out to kiss Jesus goodbye. She whispered something to Jesus that made him smile at her. With that, they climbed the mountain until they were out of sight.

Good Ol' Sam is an adaptation for clowns of the Good Samaritan story. Here, the Levite passes by the wounded man.

Good Ol' Sam

A play for clowns adapted from Luke 10; the Good Samaritan. Ordinary Time.

Themes Neighbors, helping, kindness, and giving

Rehearsal Requirement Two hours one day prior to the liturgy. A half hour-brush-up rehearsal one hour before Mass. Allow one hour to do make-up. (See Appendix.)

Characters (all dressed as clowns with make-up)
Store Owner
3 Robbers (also Innkeepers)
Priest
Levite
Sam
Donkey
Narrator

Props 1 carrot
4' thick hemp rope
2' square cardboard box
chaise lounge chair

Staging Donkey, Sam, and Store Owner are back stage at right side. All others are back stage at left. Donkey has the rope about his neck and the cardboard box is tied to his back. The chaise lounge chair is opened and sitting at left stage. The Store Owner has the carrot in his pocket. Donkey enters at right stage area and stands there in a hunched over position. Store Owner enters to load supplies on his donkey.

Narrator Jesus told this story to a young person questioning him about neighbors: It was still dark in the little town of Jerusalem. A Store Owner had just finished his breakfast and went out to the stable to load up his donkey. He was going to a town some fifty miles away just over the mountain. He needed supplies for his store; everything was low. He was a very successful store owner and everyone bought stuff from his store.

He tied down some supplies that he hoped to sell and trade in the other town. The sun was up now and he began to lead his donkey down the road. But he forgot something.

Donkey bucks and pulls.

Narrator	But his donkey didn't forget. Finally the Store Owner remembered the carrot his wife gave him for his donkey.
	After the donkey receives the carrot, he follows along. Store Owner leads him to front stage, just in front of the altar.
Narrator	He patted him on the head and they began their shopping trip. It was a twelve hour walk and he wanted to get the earliest start possible. He decided to take the shortcut over the mountain. Together, they began their climb.
	He didn't know it, but on the other side of the mountain, three robbers were coming up to meet him. They wanted his donkey, his supplies, and his money. The robbers waited quietly behind a big rock. The store owner's donkey began pulling back again. It was as if he knew something was wrong.
	Robbers enter from left stage and hide behind the altar. The robbers sit next to the chaise lounge chair facing away from the audience.
Narrator	Then, when the leader of the robbers felt the time was right, he yelled. They all jumped out on the Store Owner. The Store Owner didn't have a chance. They beat him to the ground with sticks and clubs, took his money and donkey and left him almost dead.
	Store Owner lays on his back at front stage. Priest enters and circles behind altar and comes around the altar the same way that the Store Owner did. He passes by as narration indicates and exits at left stage.
Narrator	All was quiet as he lay there bleeding to death. He was all alone; suffering by himself. He was too weak to even crawl back to town. He waited. He just about gave up hope when he heard someone coming. He was too weak even to yell. It was a priest with his hands folded in prayer. His eyes were closed too as he prayed. By chance he opened one eye and saw the dying man. How sad, he thought. But he couldn't stop tonight, or he would be late for his prayer service. He felt that someone else would come by and help him; someone who wouldn't be as busy as he. So he quietly slipped by and went his way.
	The Levite enters as priest did. He passes by as narration indicates and exits at left stage as if vomiting.
Narrator	The store owner thought that this was the end. But wait, he heard more footsteps. Could it be that the priest was returning? No. It was someone else coming by: a Levite (they are men who helped out in the Jewish church). Now he would surely help. The Levite stopped and saw the suffering man. How terrible it looked to him. He thought, "That sick man should be home in bed." But then he thought he would be sick at the sight of so much blood and dirt. So, he ran along home to get well himself.
	Sam enters at right stage with the donkey. Sam's hands are on the donkey's shoulders as he is next to him simulating riding him. They come to the front stage as the Store Owner did. He acts out the narration and places the Store Owner in *his* position on the donkey. With his arm around the Store Owner and holding the donkey's rope, he leads them to the chaise lounge chair.
Narrator	The Store Owner was ready to die now. He was thinking his last thoughts when a man approached. The Store Owner saw him. It was a man from

Samaria, a Samaritan. His name was Sam. The Store Owner hated these men and he knew he wouldn't help him. So the Store Owner said his last prayers and fainted. Then, Sam went over to him. "How come no one has helped this helpless man?", he thought to himself, "I hope I'm not too late." He got some oil and wine from his donkey and knelt next to the store owner. He cleaned up his cuts and gently placed him on his own donkey. They went down the road together.

The three robbers, now Innkeepers, rise to greet the two and their donkey. They take the Store Owner and lay him in the chaise lounge chair. Sam and donkey exit at left stage.

Narrator   They came to a warm-looking inn. Sam helped the Store Owner down and gave him to the innkeeper and his assistants. "Give him a good bed and room for the night. And a good meal, too." said Sam. "Here's the money. If there is any more money due, I'll pay you on my return trip." "Wait just a minute," said the Innkeeper, "you're a Samaritan." "That is correct," answered Sam. "You people are no good, they say," continued the Innkeeper. "Why are you doing all this for a man you don't even know? And, who knows, he may not even pay you back when he gets well."

Sam said, "The man was dying. And he is my neighbor, so I helped my neighbor." "Neighbor?" said the Innkeeper, "Ha, no one calls you Samaritans their neighbor. You guys are hated." "Well, he is my neighbor." And with that Sam gave the Innkeeper some more money and left. The Innkeeper scratched his head, looked at the money and went back into the inn to care for the Store Owner.

Special Note

1   Because clowns are associated with children and balloons, a good altar banner can be made from balloons. Get several helium-filled balloons tied to a brick or two, or three, or four. During the Offertory, bring these balloons first to be placed upon the altar for the Liturgy of the Eucharist. Tape nametags to them beforehand: Good Neighbors, Jesus, God, Spirit, Us, etc.

2   The celebrant should carry out at least one balloon during the dismissal rite.

3   A good gift to give the children in addition to the handout (see Appendix) is a free balloon. Announce that after Mass the clowns will be giving out free balloons.

4   A unique Prayer of the Faithful (Petitions) that we used to letter a prayer on a 4"x 7" card. Tape it to a helium-filled balloon. Tie the balloon to a brick. During the Entrance Rite have several clowns carry them down with the Lectionary. Place them around the pulpit. Since the children are still in the sanctuary, just after the homily, do the Prayer: One child is asked to pull down one of the balloons and read the prayer. All respond. Then give out the handouts as the children are dismissed back to their pews.

5 + 2 = 5000

A play for audience participation adapted from John 6:1 – 15; miracle of five loaves and two fishes. Ordinary Time.

Themes	Sharing, Eucharist, trust, and power of Jesus
Rehearsal Requirement	None
Characters	Jesus (should be the celebrant wearing a hooded alb) Disciple (adult with no special attire) Little Girl
Props	Coupons (enough for children in attendance, see Preparation) A colorful lunch box 2 — 1' x 2' posters as follows:

$$5 + 2 = \underline{}$$

$$\text{WITH JESUS} \qquad 5 + 2 = 5000$$

Staging   None

Preparation   Several weeks before the liturgy contact a local fast-food place. Talk to them about the play, and the publicity they will receive. Then ask them if they will supply you with 300 (or however many you will need for each child attending) coupons for one free hamburger at their place. We have never had to ask twice yet. They will jump at the chance. Ask the help of a second-grade girl. She will carry the lunch box with the coupons inside. She will take her place in the center of the crowd, which will be in the sanctuary soon. The posters are lying on the altar.

If you cannot memorize the following lines, it is better to ad-lib the general idea rather than to use hand-held cards. The children will make you feel at ease.

(The disciple enters the sanctuary. Jesus comes down to greet him.)

Disciple	Children, here we are near Jerusalem. That's where Jesus is today. Here he comes now. We've all been following him for six hours now; since before breakfast. None of us have eaten yet and it's very hot out. Come children, let's sit around Jesus again to hear him speak. Come on, come up. Come on up here, let's sit around Jesus.
	Pause, and help the children come up. Place the little girl with the lunch box in the center.
Jesus	God bless you, children. You have been following me all day.
Disciple	Lord, we are all hungry. We'd better tell them to go home to eat.
Jesus	No, let them stay. We'll feed them.
Disciple	But, Lord, we have little money, and besides, there must be five thousand people here. We can't feed all these.
Jesus	There, a little girl will share her lunch with us.
	(Disciple gets the lunch box and opens it up to show Jesus.)
Disciple	No way, Lord. Just look inside. There's only five loaves of bread and two fishes. That won't even feed you and me.
Jesus	This will feed all of us if we ask the Father's blessing.
Disciple	That's impossible, Lord.
	Disciple picks up poster "5 + 2 = _____."
Disciple	Look, five loaves of bread plus two fishes cannot equal five thousand meals for all these people. Tell them to go home, they'll get mad.
Jesus	(with outstretched hands.) Let me bless this meal. Now pass this meal around.
Disciple	But, Lord! Kids, who knows the answer to this problem? (Pause to accept the answers.) See Lord, this will not feed five thousand.
Jesus	Trust me. Pass it out.
Disciple	(passing out the coupons) Children, Jesus asked me to pass these seven items of food out among all of you. It is actually five coupons and two coupons for a free hamburger from _____ just down the street. Jesus said it'll be enough for all of you. Here, I'll pass out all I have in this lunch box until I run out.
	(Pass them out to all the children.)
Jesus	Now everyone will eat. And look, here are leftovers. We will share these with still others who are hungry for my food.
Disciple	But, Lord. There was enough for all these five thousand children. We only started with 5 and 2. It's a miracle! (Holding up the other poster) With Jesus, 5 + 2 can equal 5000. With only five loaves and two fishes we fed five thousand people. Thank you, Lord, for feeding all of us. It's a miracle, kids! Don't you want to thank Jesus? (Pause for response.)
	Jesus nods and raises his hands to bless the children.
Disciple	Lord, we love you, we want to follow you as much as we can. And we want to eat your food and trust in you. We are very thankful for having you as our friend.

Jesus and the Children

A play for mimes adapted from Matthew 19:13 – 15; Jesus blesses the children. Ordinary Time.

Themes Innocence, purity, and the Kingdom of God

Rehearsal Requirement Two hours one day prior to the liturgy.

Characters (See Appendix: Quick make-up)
Jesus (regular mime make-up)
Peter (regular mime make-up)
John (regular mime make-up)
Matthew (regular mime make-up)
2 Mothers (regular mime make-up)
Black Girl (black oval face only)
Yellow Boy (yellow oval face only)
White Girl (white oval face only)
Red Boy (red oval face only)
Nothing Boy (regular oval face with tear lines)
Narrator (adult)

Props 1 chair covered with a blanket (symbolizes a rock)
1 large tree branch with leaves (from the woods)
5 children's toys (hobby horse, hoppity Donald Duck, scooter)

Staging The chair is placed at center stage. The tree branch is tied to the back of it. The blanket is thrown over the chair. Jesus, with disciples, Peter, John, and Matthew, enter at left stage. Disciples stay at left stage while Jesus sits in the chair. Disciples slowly move to left-front stage area and sit.

Narrator It was the hottest day on record around Jerusalem today. Jesus and his friends were walking from Nazareth since early morning. All but Peter, John, and Matthew had stopped to rest as Jesus went on. Jesus had preached to the people all along the way. But now he had to rest. He saw a cool spot ahead. He told his disciples that he would rest on the rock under the tree, just up the next hill. They agreed with Jesus that he needed to rest. Jesus went up the hill and Peter, John, and Matthew found their own place to rest just below. It was a good time to rest for the crowds were far behind.

Enter two mothers with Black and White girls, Yellow, Red and Nothing Boys at left stage. They slowly move around the outside of the stage area to front stage. The children have, and are playing with or riding their toys. Disciples stop them at front stage as they try to get to Jesus. who wakes up and merely observes with a smile.

Narrator Some mothers with their playful children were trying to catch up to Jesus all day. They always seemed to just miss him. But finally they could see Jesus atop the next hill. All the mothers wanted was for Jesus to touch and bless their children. But the children wanted to play all the time; that's why they couldn't catch up. But now, Jesus was in sight. They quickly gathered their children together and hurried up the hill.

Narrator The disciples saw them coming. They knew how tired Jesus was and ran over to stop them. "Stop," they yelled as they scared the children, "Go away! The master is tired. He doesn't have time for you kids. You wouldn't understand his great words anyway. Go away now, he doesn't have time for kids."

Children start away but the two mothers stop them. They organize them again and encounter the disciples a second time.

Narrator The children were scared and started back down the hill. But their mothers traveled too far to give up now. So, they got the children together and faced up to the disciples again. "We want the Master to bless our kids," they pleaded.

Disciples point away firmly.

Narrator "No!" the disciples screamed, "Leave now!"

They turn away dejected. Jesus sits up attentively as he raises his hands toward the disciples, letting them know that he wishes to speak. Kids drop toys and run to sit around Jesus. As their time to speak comes up, they kneel up above the other children. Mothers and disciples gather up toys and sit behind the children.

Narrator They gave up and were leaving when Jesus called out to his disciples, "Let the little children come to me." Jesus was displeased with his disciples, but as the children came running, he smiled again. He looked at the disciples again and said, "Don't you know that the Kingdom of God belongs to such as these? Anyone who will not come to God as a little child will never be allowed into his Kingdom."

The children began to ask Jesus questions. They loved to listen to him speak. One little girl spoke up first. "I am a Black girl, sir. I've traveled all this way to see you. Sir, some say I can't find God. Can I, sir?" Jesus put his hand on her head and said, "You're going the right way, little Black girl. God is surely with you now."

Another boy spoke up: "Sir, I'm a Yellow boy from far away. Does God love me too?" Jesus smiled as he whispered, "God is your Father, little Yellow boy. And he loves you as much as he loves me, his Son."

With that the other girl questioned him: "Sir, I'm a White girl and I like you. But I've been told that I can't understand you." Jesus touched her shoulder and said, "You understand me better than most older people. And God names you one of his children."

Another boy interrupted and said: "But, sir, I'm a Red boy. If God loves all of these kids, do you think he can love me, too?" Jesus took him by the hands and said, "Just as I invite you to be loved by me, so does the Father invite you to his love. He does love you just as he loves all his children."

The other little boy was very shy and bashful. Jesus turned to him and said, "And what about you little boy. Don't you have a question?" "I guess so, sir," the little boy answered. "I am an orphan. I have no father or mother. I have no brothers or sisters. I was found abandoned by the roadside when I was a baby. I am a nothing boy; not Black, White, Yellow, or Red. Can God love me?"

Jesus sat back and then spoke, "You, my little Nothing Boy, are loved. God is your father and mother and I am your brother and sister. All of these are your brothers and sisters. You are not a Nothing Boy. You are a child of God and that makes you a Something Boy. You are definitely loved."

Jesus rises and places his hands on the children's heads. They all smile, and they rise with Jesus and hug him as he leaves with his disciples at right stage. Children and mothers exit at left stage.

Narrator   Then Jesus rose up and blessed all the children. As he took them into his arms, they all smiled as if they shared a secret that the older people didn't know yet. Jesus said goodbye and continued on with his disciples. Then the children, with their toys, left to go back home with their mothers. And they were still smiling about the secret they shared with Jesus.

Ten Little Lepers

A play for mimes adapted from Luke 17:11 – 19; one leper returned to say "Thank You." Ordinary Time.

Themes	Thanking, cleansing, giving, and receiving, appreciation, forgiving, and reconciliation
Rehearsal Requirement	Two hours one day prior to the liturgy. A one-half hour brush-up an hour before Mass is advisable.
Characters	Priest (also plays disciple) 3 Townspeople (also play disciples) Jesus Jack 9 Lepers Narrator
Props	10 hand bells (for lepers to ring) 20 rags (approximately 12" long to be tied on forearms of lepers) 20—4" squares of posterboard tags (2 are numbered 1, 2 are numbered 2, up to 10). These are tied to the lepers' arms just above the elbow.

```
1    2    3    4
1    2    3    4
```

... and so on until
```
9    10
9    10
```

Staging   Lepers 1 – 9 have number and rags on their arms and bells in hand. Leper #1 holds Jack's #10 tags. Lepers are at left back stage while all others are at right back stage. Jack and Priest enter and go to front stage where they sit. Priest has Jack's rags and bell. Jack lowers head in tears as Priest ties his rags on him and gives him his bell.

Narrator   There once was a young man named Jack. He was a good husband and had three good children. He was the leader of his town, and everyone liked Jack. The town priest came to see Jack. But, today, the priest was sad as he sat down with Jack. The priest didn't sit close to Jack as he used to; he was careful not to even touch Jack. Jack knew something was very wrong.

"Jack," said the priest, "you must leave this town. You have the worst disease ever—leprosy. You can't stay with the people any longer. Here, you must keep your sores wrapped at all times. And it'll get worse. Soon your whole body will be covered with sores. And you must ring this bell whenever you see people coming near you. That will tell them to stay away from you because you are unclean. You must go to live by yourself in the caves up in the hills."

Priest goes to right stage area where he meets townspeople. Jack rings bell and walks toward right stage but is chased to left stage. Priest and towns-people exit at right stage.

Narrator   "Leave now! Get out of town," the priest continued. Jack just cried as the priest returned back to town. He thought of his family, and of his little town. He wondered if he could go back just for one last "goodbye." So, he tried to go back while ringing his leper bell. He saw his best friend, Harry. But Harry hid from Jack. Then he saw his brother and sister. They saw Jack coming and shouted at him, "Get away! You're unclean. Get away!"

Jack cried some more as he saw the priest. He asked if he might just get his suitcase. The priest pointed for Jack to leave as some of the townspeople threw stones at him. And poor little Jack left, alone, with no food and crying again. He was very sad and didn't feel like a whole man any longer.

Enter 9 lepers at left stage. They march outside the stage area from left stage to front stage to right stage as Jack watches. They are ringing their bells. They continue marching to center stage where Jack comes over to them. They give Jack his #10 tags, tie them to his arms, and all sit.

Narrator   Jack was still crying when he got to the caves in the hills. He saw nine people coming toward him. They were ringing bells too. They were also wrapped with leper rags. At first he was going to hide from them, but then he realized that he was a leper too. He wondered if they would let him live with them. He went over to them, but, before he could ask, they spoke: "Hi, Jack," the first leper said, "you must live with us." Jack felt a little better to have some other people to live with. The first leper continued, "Here, Jack, we are nine lepers. But now you will make us ten lepers. Now come join us in our cave. Have some of our food while we talk."

Lepers mime as narration continues. They merely take turns extending hands to one another, slowly, as they speak.

Narrator They all told their own stories to Jack. All of them cried because they wanted to go home. They liked their leper friends, but they still felt sad. They cleansed their sores and ate together. Jack noticed that his sores were now spreading to his legs and face. He cried as the other lepers helped him.

Narrator One leper spoke up: "Tomorrow, this Jesus of Nazareth may pass by. They say he raised people who were dead and gave sight to blind people. Maybe he can cure us." Jack's eyes opened wide.

Jack kneels up in prayer as others lay back in sleep. Then Jack lies back.

Narrator The others slept as he prayed to God. He asked if he and the other lepers might be cured tomorrow. Then he slept.

Enter Jesus and disciples at right stage. They walk to front stage where lepers converge on them. Disciples back off in fear as Jesus greets the lepers.

Narrator All of them were sleeping soundly. All except Jack. He heard voices and rose to see. It was Jesus and his disciples. He woke up his leper friends and they began to run to Jesus. His disciples shouted, "Stay away, you lepers! Stay away! Unclean." But Jesus opened his arms to greet them. He told his disciples to be quiet.

Lepers line up in numerical order in front of Jesus. They should be lined up from right stage to front stage so the audience can see the action. Disciples come up to help the lepers. Jesus unties their rags and lets them drop. He takes their bells and drops them too. Lepers gather at left stage.

Narrator "Come here," he said, "I will heal you." They lined up as Jesus unwrapped their bandages. He started with the first leper and he was healed. The second leper cried as his bandages were thrown to the ground. He was clean. Jack was peering over the line as he waited his turn. He was very excited and happy again.

Jesus continued healing the lepers. His disciples were so shocked at this miracle that they came over to help. They were all together. They were all smiling as the bandages and bells were thrown to the ground. One, two, three lepers healed. Four, five, six lepers cured. Seven, eight, nine lepers made clean. And ten lepers once again happy. They were all gathered together laughing as Jesus turned to them.

Jesus raises his arms to lepers. Lepers exit in a hurry at left stage. Jack returns after he exits. He goes to Jesus and hugs him and then exits at left stage. Jesus and disciples exit at right stage.

Narrator "You are now blessed and healed," he said. "All of you look better. Just look at your clean bodies. Now, go back into your towns and show the priest that you are healed."

They all ran to town as Jesus and his disciples began to go on. But Jack remembered his prayer the night before. Jack came running back yelling "Jesus, Jesus, thanks for healing me."

Jesus took Jack by the arms, looked at his disciples, and said, "Was not

God's gift given to ten? Where are the others? Of all those men only Jack returned to thank God. Go home, Jack, your body looks better, but you alone will feel better."

Jack ran home to the priest, his wife, and three good children. All the way home he smiled. He was healed. He was cured. He was a whole man again.

Special Note

1   A good Entrance Rite is to have no song. Have the celebrant enter alone ringing a leper's bell.

2   Bring up the rags and bells with the Offertory gifts to be placed around the top of the altar. This is a good visual for children to understand that the Eucharist heals and unites all God's people too.

Mimes portray the ten lepers as they are being cured.

A Roadside Miracle
(for Bartimaeus)

A play for costumed players with speaking parts adapted from Mark 10:46 – 52. Ordinary Time.

Themes	Healing, everyone matters to Jesus, trust, and individualism
Rehearsal Requirement	Two hours one day prior to the liturgy with one-half hour brush-up just before Mass.
Characters	Bart (dressed as a beggar) Jesus (dressed in an alb) 5 Crowd People (dressed in contemporary clothing) Narrator
Props	None
Staging	Bart enters dressed as a beggar with sunglasses and a walking stick. He goes to front stage stumbling until he falls and sits down. He faces away from the stage area.

Narrator	There once was a blind beggar named Bartimaeus. Bart always came to this place at the roadside to beg for money and food. He couldn't work because no one would hire a blind man. And many people who came down this road would spit or throw stones at Bart. But the roadside belonged to Bart and he wasn't about to leave. Where would he go? He's blind. So here Bartimaeus sat. Then he heard voices coming. Enter crowd people who gather at center stage. They mumble while moving around constantly.
Narrator	A large crowd gathered on the road. Bart extended his hand.
Bart	Please help a poor blind man. Can you give me some food, or a few pennies?
Crowd Person 1	Shut up, old fool. Don't bother us. You're a nobody. You don't fit in with us.
Narrator	Bart tried to hear what they were mumbling about. Bart strains to hear them.
Narrator	He heard one person say that Jesus was coming by today. Bart knew of this

Jesus. He knew he was God's Son and could cure people. He sat, and kept his ears opened.

Jesus enters and walks slowly from right stage to left stage at the back stage wall. His attention is to himself only until Bart yells.

Narrator Jesus had just left Jericho and was traveling the road to Jerusalem. He knew that the people who hated him enough to kill him were in Jerusalem. But, sadly, he knew that God wanted him to go into Jerusalem. He was thinking of what was waiting for him there, when the crowd began yelling at him. He was too sad to really hear them. His thoughts were on Jerusalem. His eyes were fixed down the road on the city gates of Jerusalem—where Jesus would die.

Crowd Person 1 Jesus, miracle worker, I'm poor. Make me a rich king. Do a miracle for me.

Crowd Person 2 Master, some hate me and have killed my family. Do one of your miracles for me. Make me a strong soldier so I can kill them.

Crowd Person 3 Lord, make me rich.

Crowd Person 4 Messiah, give me gold, silver, and a big castle.

Crowd Person 5 Son of Man, give me land. Make people follow me. Make me a great leader.

Bart (Yelling loudly) Jesus, Son of David, have pity on me!

Crowd turns to Bart. Jesus takes notice, stops walking and turns.

All Crowd Shhhhhhhhhh!

Crowd Person 2 Be quiet old fool. You're not one of us. You're a nobody. Be quiet!

Jesus takes a few steps toward center stage. Crowd turns to Jesus again and starts throwing requests at him again. Bart with hands held high yells again.

Bart Son of David, have pity on me!

Jesus Call him over.

All crowd people kneel. Crowd Person 2 goes to Bart and leads him to Jesus.

Crowd Person 2 Get up old fool. He is calling you. Do not fear; it is Jesus.

Bart kneels at Jesus' feet. Crowd Person 2 kneels with crowd. Jesus touches Bart's head and exits at left stage.

Jesus What do you want me to do for you?

Bart Lord Jesus, I want to see.

Jesus Be on your way. Your faith has healed you.

Narrator And with that Jesus left him. Bart was too scared to open his eyes. But then, he did. And he could see!

Bart turns to crowd, throws off his glasses, and excitedly touches the crowd people. He is yelling that he can see. The crowd rises and pats Bart happily. They all exit at left stage.

Narrator   Bart was so happy. A simple miracle by the roadside was his. All he had to do was ask. He looked for Jesus and saw that he was gone. He ran after him and the crowd followed them into Jerusalem. Bart could see; he was no longer blind. A simple roadside miracle happened today, Jesus' roadside miracle for Bartimaeus.

In this scene from *5 + 2 = 5000,* parish youngsters gather in the sanctuary and watch as Jesus speaks to a disciple.

When Are You Coming Again, Jesus?

A play for mimes adapted from Mark 13:24 – 37. Ordinary Time—Advent.

Themes   Waiting, preparation, future, and present times

Rehearsal Requirement   Two hours one day prior to the liturgy. A one-half hour brush-up before Mass.

Characters

Jesus
Disciple
Angel
Sun
Moon
Stars (one person who also plays the angel)
Son of Man (also plays the fig tree)
Narrator

Props

Cassette tape recorder/player
Tape of a trumpet blasting
A large sun (drawn on a posterboard one side yellow, the other blue)
A large sun (drawn on a posterboard one side brown, the other black)
A large moon (drawn on a posterboard one side white, the other blue)
A large moon (drawn on a posterboard one side brown, the other black)
4 large stars made from aluminum foil
A 6' tree branch with several yellow and brown construction paper leaves taped to it
A white sheet (for the Son of Man's clouds of glory)

Staging   The suns are laid on the floor at center stage. The moons are laid next to them two feet away. The four stars are lying in front of the suns and moons. The tree branch is lying at right stage. Enter Jesus and disciple from left stage; all others are at right stage. They extend a hand to one another as they speak. When Jesus speaks, he holds up his hand to the disciple and then slowly swings it around to center stage as they both sit.

Narrator   One day a disciple asked Jesus a very scarey question: "Hey, Jesus, what's it going to be like at the end of the world?" Jesus just looked at him and said, "Are you sure you want to ask that?" He nodded yes. Jesus spoke:

Enter Sun and Moon to center stage. Sun raises his yellow sun first; in a circular fashion from left to right. As he comes around full circle back to the floor, he turns it to blue and circles that. Then, down to the floor again, he raises the brown sun, and finally he raises the black sun and holds it high as he takes a few steps back. Moon does the same with white, blue, brown, then black. They should synchronize their circular movements so that the sun is at its top while the moon is at the floor. They remain standing in the background holding their black sun and moon high.

Jesus During that time after all kinds of troubles here on earth, the sun and moon will grow darker and darker. After a few days they will lose some of their light. Then after a few weeks they will get darker yet until several months pass by and they will shine no more. They will disappear to everyone's sight. They will be black in the sky; just dead, cold rocks in the heavens. And the earth will have no light; she will have no warmth for her cold endless nights. Her sun and moon will be gone forever.

Enter Stars to center stage, who raises the four stars high, shakes them, and violently throws them down to the floor. She stoops to the floor and crawls to right stage to become the angel.

Jesus And the stars, the millions of stars in the heavens will be shaken above. They will roll in the skies until they collide with one another. And the stars, also, after weeks and months will be shaken so hard that they will fall out of the sky; every one until they are no more.

Enter Son of Man to center stage. He has a white sheet about his shoulders and clutched in his hands. He should let his arms move slowly outward to allow the sheet to bellow and flow. He motions to the angel as the tape of the trumpet blast plays. Angel dances across the stage to the first row of the audience. She gathers a few children and ushers them to sit at front stage looking at the Son of Man, who moves closer to them. Angel comes up to Son of Man and she, Sun, Moon and Stars all sit facing away from audience. Son of Man drops his sheet and goes to right stage where he sits by tree branch.

Jesus Then, the Son of Man will appear in the sky; it will be beautiful. He will ride on great white clouds with power and glory. He will have his angels with him. And he'll send one angel with a great trumpet blast (tape here) and she'll go out into the four winds of the earth to gather up the chosen people. She'll gather every good girl and boy no matter how old or young they are; no matter where they are. Under her wing they will come and see the Son of Man, and they will be with him in all his glory in heaven. The angel will move quickly with the wind and will not cease until all his friends are brought to him.

Disciple sits up as Jesus kneels up. Disciple sits back on his hands. Jesus again extends one hand to him and slowly swings it around to center stage as he sits back.

Narrator Well, after hearing Jesus tell him all this, the disciple sat back breathless. He was sorry that he ever asked. He took a deep breath and dared to ask another question: "Wow! Jesus, what are we going to do?" Jesus smiled and told him:

Fig Tree rises up, slowly plucks off his leaves, and lets them drop. He sits back on the floor facing away from the audience.

Jesus   Learn a lesson from the fig tree: After the fig tree grows up, sprouts her green leaves and gives up her juicy fruit, her leaves turn yellow and brown until they all fall off. And you see this sign of the fig tree and know that Winter is coming soon. So you prepare for Winter.

Disciple and Jesus rise up to their feet again.

Jesus   So I say to you, my disciple, keep watch, be prepared every day for the coming of the Son of Man. Do things right now to prepare.

Narrator   The disciple was feeling better now since his first question. So he tried yet another question: "How can I figure out exactly when all of this will happen?"

Jesus puts one arm around the disciple's shoulder.

Jesus   As to the exact hour or day, no one knows it, neither the angels in heaven nor even the Son, but only the Father.

Narrator   You think the disciple's curiosity would have been satisfied by now. But no, he had to ask still one more question: "Will everything on this earth come to an end?"

Jesus waves his free arm slowly across front, right and center stage in a sweeping motion. As he does this all the mimes still on stage exit at right stage. Jesus then walks off with the disciple at left stage.

Narrator   Jesus smiled one more time and answered this questioning disciple:

Jesus   The heavens and earth will pass away—all disappear, pass away, out of sight. But my words will not pass away. So keep watch, prepare now every minute. I want you all to be ready.

Special Note

1   If you have special lighting capabilities, it is very effective to flash or dim them during the early part of the play.

2   If you have a good trumpet player, it is better to have a real trumpet blast than a mere tape.

Look Out Below!

A play for mimes and clowns adapted from Luke 5:17 – 27; a paralyzed man cured. Advent.

Themes   Ingenuity, determination, friendship, healing, and faith

Rehearsal Requirement   Two hours one day prior to the liturgy with one-half hour brush-up just before Mass.

Characters
Tiny Tom (a skinny second-grader mime)
Zeek and Zak (two big, strong eighth-grader clowns)
Jesus (a mime)
Two Pharisees (mimes)
Two Teachers (mimes)
Two Scribes (mimes)
Narrator

Props   Two chairs

Staging   Two chairs are at center right stage area. Tom, Zeek, and Zack are at left stage, others are at right. Enter Tom who lays on his back at center left stage area. He is motionless except for his head. He raises his head to see who's coming.

Narrator   There was a young man named Tiny Tom. He got that nickname from his friends because he was so small. Tiny Tom was paralyzed from his neck down; the only thing he could move was his head. He had a terrible accident when he was a baby and none of the many doctors or magicians could fix him up. He even stopped growing. Not one person could cure him; and they tried for several years now. They gave him up for hopeless. And Tiny Tom gave himself up for hopeless too. He felt that he was no good to anyone; he couldn't do anything but talk. He was very sad today because his friends went to a party and he was alone. Then, he heard voices coming.

Enter Zeek and Zack. Zeek lifts Tom's head and shoulders and props him up in his lap. Zack raises his hand as he speaks. Zeek uses one hand and his head as he speaks to Tom.

Narrator   It was his only friends, Zeek and Zack. These two funny guys would visit Tiny Tom periodically to cheer him up. They were real clowns and could make Tiny Tom forget his troubles and laugh. They were a crazy sort and even worse today. They grabbed Tiny Tom in excitement; they were always touching Tiny Tom, lifting him up, and holding his dead little hands. They

---

treated Tiny Tom as if he weren't paralyzed at all. Zack began to tell Tiny Tom his news:

"As we were going to the party we heard a great voice coming from the church. We listened a while and heard a man say that it was a great prophet named Jesus."

Tiny Tom secretly wished he could walk so he might get out of the house to hear Jesus. He heard about this Jesus and had come to believe in him. He heard of his healing sick people, giving sight to blind people and raising the dead back to life. He wondered if he could be cured by Jesus. But he couldn't walk or even crawl to get to Jesus. So, he hopelessly put it out of his mind.

Zeek and Zack pick up Tom. Jesus, Pharisees, Teachers, and Scribes enter to center right stage area just in front of the two chairs. They all sit close together in a line facing Jesus, miming a discussion. Zeek and Zack fumble around, all over the stage, while trying to carry Tom to Jesus.

Narrator   But Zeek and Zack didn't put it out of their minds. They knew what they were going to do. They grabbed Tiny Tom and carried him out of the room, out of the house and onto the city streets. Tiny Tom was shocked; they never acted this way before. They never carried him outside. He wasn't even allowed outside.

"What's going on?" Tiny Tom shouted. "Put me down you crazy clowns! Watch out for that puddle! Look out for that horse! What's going on?" But his screams did no good. Zeek and Zack had something on their minds for their little helpless friend, and there was no stopping them until they completed their task.

Tiny Tom saw the church at the end of the street. His heart raced as he hoped that that was where Zeek and Zack were headed. He began to hear a beautiful voice coming from the little church building. Tiny Tom felt something he hadn't felt for years now—hope. He knew Jesus could cure him if his friends could just get him inside.

They are at the line of Pharisees, Teachers, and Scribes by now. They try to get by them but fall back several times.

Narrator   Their hearts beat faster; they could all hear Jesus very clearly now. They could almost see him over the crowd of Pharisees, Teachers, and Scribes who came to hear him speak. "They tried to bring him in and lay him before Jesus; but they found no way of getting him through because of the crowd."

Tiny Tom felt hopelessness coming back into his heart. He began to give up again. But not Zeek and Zack; they didn't carry their tiny friend all this way to go back the same way; carrying him. They left Tiny Tom on the sidewalk.

Zeek and Zack walk around the crowd on opposite sides. They bump into each other behind the chairs and fall down. They slowly turn to notice the chairs. They climb upon them and peer in over Jesus. They jump for joy and fall off their chairs, brush themselves off, and run to get Tom.

Narrator   Zeek and Zack looked all around the little church building to see if there was a side door. They came around back and after they bumped into each other they saw a ladder leading up to the straw and tile roof. They climbed up and peeked through the roof. Both of them jumped for joy. They jumped so high that they fell off the roof. But that didn't stop their joy. They got right up and ran around to Tiny Tom.

Zeek and Zack lift Tom and carry him around to the back. They stand on the chairs and lower Tom by his wrists to Jesus. They stay standing and watching from the roof. Jesus rises and lays Tom at his feet.

Narrator Zack told Tiny Tom something that made his heart have hope again: "We're going to get you in and lay you in the Master's lap." Tiny Tom thought that they found a side entrance and was full of joy. Zeek and Zack lifted Tiny Tom again and fumbled around to the back. When they began to climb the ladder Tiny Tom began to scream again, "What's going on? Are you clowns crazy? We're going to all be killed? What's going on?" Zeek said, "We're going through the roof!"

"So they went up the roof. There they let him down with his mat through the tiles into the middle of the crowd before Jesus." Zeek and Zack began shouting as they lowered Tiny Tom through the roof, "Look out below! Coming through! Heads up! Look out below!" Jesus saw what was happening and caught Tiny Tom as he fell through the roof. He gently laid him at his feet. Jesus smiled as he looked up at Zeek and Zack.

Jesus stands and raises his arms to all.

Narrator "Seeing their faith," Jesus said, "My friend, your sins are forgiven you." Tiny Tom's body wasn't cured but when Jesus said, ". . . your sins are forgiven you," he felt great. It was all he wanted; to meet Jesus and know his sins were forgiven by the Son of God himself. He felt great!

Pharisees, Teachers, and Scribes kneel up to speak.

Narrator The Scribes, Teachers, and Pharisees began a discussion, saying: "Who is this man who utters blasphemies? Who can forgive sins but God alone?" Jesus, however, knew their reasoning and answered them by saying: "Why do you harbor these thoughts? Which is easier to say, 'Your sins are forgiven you,' or to say 'Get up and walk?' In any case, to make it clear to you that the Son of Man has authority on earth to forgive sins"—he addressed the paralyzed man: "I say to you, get up! Take your mat with you, and return to your house."

Tom rises up in a leap. His hands high he bursts through the crowd and goes around back. Zeek and Zack jump for joy at seeing Tom rise up. They fall off of the chairs again. Tom helps them up this time and they exit left stage arm in arm.

Narrator Tiny Tom got right up. He sang with joy and burst through the front door of the church. He remembered his friends Zeek and Zack and went around back to show them that he could walk. He found them lying in the dirt for they had fallen off the roof with such happiness. This time Tiny Tom helped them to get up and they all went home singing praises to God. Tiny Tom even said that he felt like he was growing taller already.

Crowd rises and follows Jesus off stage at right stage.

Narrator And inside the little church: "At this they were all seized with astonishment. Full of awe, they gave praise to God, saying, 'We have seen incredible things today.'" At that, Jesus left the little church to move on to another town, and they all followed him as far as they could.

Only Fifty Feet
From Christmas

A play for costumed players with speaking parts and audience singing participation.

Rehearsal Requirement Two hours one day prior to Christmas Eve. The best time for this liturgy is 4:00 P.M. Christmas Eve. It is next to impossible to have a brush-up rehearsal just before the liturgy, so merely talk it through with the children as they arrive.

Characters Speaking parts—eighth graders or older
Narrator
Innkeeper, Jebidiah (with dust rag)
Innkeeper's wife, Mabel (with dust rag)
Nonspeaking parts—second or third graders
Mary
Joseph (with walking stick)
Archangel (with sword)
6 Angels (or more)
Star Angel (with 3' aluminum-foil star on a stick)
4 Shepherds (or more)
3 Kings (with traditional gifts)
Drummer Boy (with drum)
Folk Group (to lead audience singing.)

Props Spotlight
Bale of hay
Nativity scene (children can make these 3' high, out of posterboard)
Baby doll wrapped in rags
2 windows as shown

They are made of posterboard reinforced on the back with sticks glued on. They are tied together at one side so they can stand alone in the shape of a ''V''. Paint them with bright colors.

Staging A spotlight greatly enhances this play. If it is available, spot the action as it takes place. The stage is set as ''Staging'' indicates. Joseph and Mary enter from left stage. They walk around the outside of the stage area to the opposite side of the altar. Joseph knocks on the altar.

Narrator A young man named Joseph was traveling on the evening road with his new wife, Mary. They walked from Nazareth eighty miles away. Joseph was

70

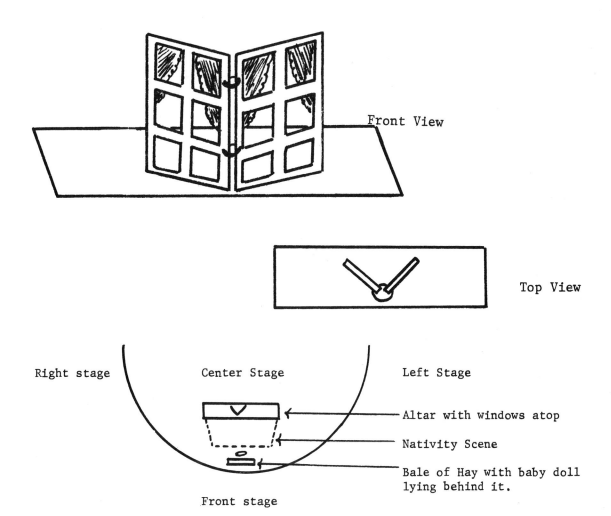

Front View

Top View

Right stage   Center Stage   Left Stage

Altar with windows atop

Nativity Scene

Bale of Hay with baby doll
lying behind it.

Front stage

ordered to take his family to his birth town to be counted for the governor's census. The governor wanted to know how many people he ruled so that he could raise the taxes. Mary rode upon a little donkey and Joseph led him slowly. He didn't want Mary to fall for she was soon to have a baby. Many, many travelers passed them by during the day; they could move faster. But Joseph and Mary weren't worried. They knew that Mary's baby was God's Son and He would protect them. They arrived in Bethlehem late at night. The inns were very crowded; people were squeezed in everywhere. Joseph noticed one inn that didn't look too crowded. He went up to the door and knocked.

Enter Innkeeper, Jebidiah, from left stage. He crosses over to answer the door.

Innkeeper   (growling) Yes, what is it now? (opening the door) Not more travelers. I'm sorry we're full up. You'll have to go elsewhere, I'm really busy cleaning up and getting ready for tomorrow's breakfast.

Narrator   Joseph spoke in a soft voice as he told the Innkeeper that his wife would soon have a baby.

Innkeeper   Oh, I'm sorry, but I've got a lot on my mind too. Wait, there's a stable out

	back, about fifty feet around the side of my inn. It's dirty and smelly but it's better than having a baby in the streets.
Narrator	Joseph and Mary were pleased to have any place that had a roof. And Mary was so close to having her baby born that Joseph had no choice but to accept the stable as their shelter for the night.
Innkeeper	My wife will show you the way. I'm really too busy even for that. Mabel, Mabel! Where is that woman when you need her? Mabel!

Mabel enters from left stage and comes over to Jeb. She rubs her eyes as if awakened from a nap. She takes Mary and Joseph to the front of the hay. Mary sits on the bale while Joseph stands next to her. Jeb goes to back stage wall where he cleans whatever is there. Mabel returns through the door and cleans the altar and windows.

Mabel	Yes, Yes, what is it now? I'm tired, Jebidiah. I've been cleaning all day. We've never been this crowded before. What is it?
Innkeeper	Show these people to the stable out back. And hurry back, we've got lots to prepare for.
Mabel	What! The stable? Can't you see this woman is going to have a baby?
Innkeeper	It's either out back or out in the streets.
Narrator	Mary whispered to Mabel that they would be fine in the stable. So Mabel took them out into the night air fifty feet around the side of the inn to the stable. After she saw to it that they were as comfortable as possible, she left.
Mabel	Well, it's done. Now what do you want me to do?
Innkeeper	Just stay there and clean the tables, chairs, and especially those dirty windows. And don't be slow; there's much to prepare for. This is the best season ever. We'll get rich off this census-taking by the governor. I hope he does this every year. We could make it a holiday and get richer every year. Now, hurry, clean, and dust.
Mabel	Okay, okay.

As Mabel and Jeb dust, Mary slowly reaches behind the hay bale to get the baby doll. Folk Group leads the audience in singing the song. Mary rocks the baby doll.

Narrator	Just then, after Joseph and Mary finished unpacking, while the innkeeper and his wife cleaned, the baby was born.

First stanza and refrain of "Joy to the World" is sung. After the singing, shepherds and drummer boy enter from left stage. They go to left stage just outside the stage area. Archangel enters with them and goes to left stage. He raises his arms and sword to them. They are led to the stable by the archangel during the next song. Archangel stands behind Mary while the others kneel at random to the left stage side of Mary and Joseph. Folk group leads all in song.

Narrator	Not too far away, just over the hills of Bethlehem, shepherds were working the night shift. It was a bright star-lit night. God sent an Archangel to them in the fields. He was to announce that God's Son was born this very night. The shepherds were scared but the archangel brought them peace as he told

them the good news. And they followed God's archangel to the stable where Jesus was born. They were followed by a poor drummer boy. He also sensed that something special was happening.

First stanza and refrain of "The First Noel" is sung. Mabel watches all the action through the windows. She turns to Jeb after the singing is finished.

Mabel Jebidiah, Jebidiah!

Jeb What now? You'll do anything to get out of work. We've got a lot to do yet. What is it?

Mabel (running up to Jeb) I just saw a bright light out back near the stable. And some shepherds and a poor drummer boy followed the light. I felt real warm as they passed by.

Jeb Well, if those poor shepherds want a room, tell them we're filled up. They probably don't have the money to pay for a room anyway. We only want people who can pay here.

Mabel No, no, Jebidiah, I think they wanted to go to the stable. There must be something special happening out back.

Jeb Get back to work. We have a full house. We've got lots to do before breakfast. Now get busy! Special stuff is happening right here; we're getting rich.

Mabel (returning to the windows) I guess you're right, Jebidiah. We do have more important things to do. And our Inn is full for the first time ever.

After Mabel returns the angels enter, half from left stage and half from right—not the Star Angel. During the next song they line up next to archangel behind Joseph and Mary. They outstretch their arms until the singing stops. Folk group leads singing. Mabel looks through the window.

Narrator Then suddenly all the angels in heaven came down upon the little stable.

First stanza and refrain of "Hark! The Herald Angels Sing" is sung.

Mabel (after singing stops) Jebidiah, did you hear that? And you should have seen all the light coming from out back.

Jeb Woman, woman, get back to work. If you don't, I'll go to bed now leaving you to finish all the preparations.

Mabel No, no please, Jebidiah. I'll continue my work.

Star Angel enters from right stage. She stands there until the singing begins. Enter Three Kings who follow the Star. Star Angel lines up next to angels as kings kneel to the right stage side of Mary and Joseph. Folk group leads singing. Mabel looks thru windows.

Narrator And far, far off in the East a bright star was moving in the sky. And following her were three Kings from the Orient. They were Melchior, Caspar, and Balthasar. They came following this great star. They came with their caravans of camels.

First stanza and refrain of "We Three Kings of Orient Are" is sung.

Mabel (after singing stops) Jebidiah, you're not going to believe this.

Jeb You're probably right. What now?

Mabel	I just saw three kings go out back. And there's a great bright star over our Inn.
Jeb	I guess this crowd and all these preparations are driving you crazy. Let's go to bed. We'll have a busy day tomorrow.
Mabel	But, Jebidiah . . .
Jeb	Good night! (exits left stage)
Mabel	Wait, wait, Jebidiah. I'm coming. (exits left stage)
Narrator	And the night finally became quiet inside the innkeeper's inn. And out back, only 50 feet from the innkeeper and his wife, the night became silent and holy.

"Silent Night, Holy Night" is sung.

Special Note

1 In your bulletin insert and invitations (see Appendix) advertise asking the children to bring a Christmas gift for the poor. Arrange this with a local charity house so they can be there to receive them. Ask the children to bring one *new* article of winter clothing. Tell them to label it outside; boy or girl, size, what it is, etc.

2 The offertory song should be "The Little Drummer Boy." This is played and sung over and over until the offertory is finished.

3 During the Offertory, the celebrant sits in a chair at front stage. He is flanked by several adults. The drummer boy player leads the procession down the center aisle to the celebrant. The drummer boy goes to the Nativity Scene where he stands beating his drum until the procession is over. The children process down to the celebrant who receives their gifts. The adult helpers place the gift packages around the altar and stage.

4 Inviting the children up into the sanctuary for a homily is not advisable because you might have too many children at this liturgy. The handouts (See Appendix) should have a candy cane attached to them and be given to the children after they present their gift to the celebrant.

A Single Word

A play for costumed players and two mimes with speaking parts and audience singing participation.

Rehearsal Requirement Two hours one day prior to Christmas Eve. The best time for this liturgy is 4:00 P.M. Christmas Eve. It is next to impossible to have a brush-up rehearsal just before the liturgy so merely talk it through with the children as they arrive.

Characters Speaking parts—eighth graders or older
Narrator
God (a white-faced mime dressed in a white alb)
Devil (a red-faced mime)
Nonspeaking parts—second or third graders
Mary
Joseph
Archangel (with sword in one hand)
4 Shepherds (or more)
3 Kings
6 Angels (or more)
Star Angel (with 3' aluminum-foil star)
Folk Group (to lead audience singing)

Props Spotlight
1 chair
White rag (to gag God)
Bale of hay
Nativity scene (children can make these 3' high, out of posterboard)
Baby doll wrapped in rags

Staging The staging is the same as in Only Fifty Feet from Christmas. The only addition is the one chair, which is placed just behind the center of the altar. The only deletion is the windows atop the altar—not used in this play.

See "Staging" to set up. A spotlight greatly enhances this play. If it is available, spot the action as it takes place. Enter God with gag tied about his mouth. He is led by the devil to stand upon the chair at the altar. Devil prances around God in jest.

Narrator Somehow, about a million years ago the devil was able to gag God. That's right, he was able to get a magic cloth wrapped around God's mouth. God couldn't get it off. As a matter of fact, he didn't even try to get it off. God couldn't speak—not a single word. The devil was very happy. He danced around God making fun of him. He was glad God hadn't tried to take it off.

The devil leaves God and goes to left stage running with his one arm out. He moves up and down from left stage to front stage to right stage. Then he goes back to prance around God.

Narrator   Finally, the devil tired of teasing God. He left God and went out into the earth. He saw two people in a beautiful garden. It was a man named Adam and a woman named Eve. They were too happy. So the devil changed into a snake and made them eat a poisoned apple. The devil laughed, for he knew God forbid these people to eat of this tree. Pleased with his work on Adam and Eve, the devil flew back to heaven to tell God. He danced around our poor silent God, chanting to him:

"They listened to my words.
They ate the apple.
You cannot speak to them.
They are mine forever.
Look now, they have children in pain."

The devil leaves God, moves around the stage as before, and returns to God again.

Narrator   The devil left God again, when he saw Adam and Eve's children. He went into one child, Cain, and caused him to hate his brother, Abel. He whispered into Cain's ear that Abel was out to get him. He told Cain to kill Abel and Cain did as the Devil said. The devil was happy. He danced up to heaven to see God again.

"Look God," he sang, "your children are killing one another. Cain has killed Abel. He hears me and listens. And you are silent. God can't speak while his children are killing each other. God is silent." The devil saw hundreds and thousands of God's people in Egypt.

The devil leaves God to circle stage and return as before.

Narrator   Thousands of years went by, and still God couldn't speak from the devil's trickery. God almost cried when he saw the devil going after His favorite people, the Israelites. They were in Egypt living happily. But God couldn't speak. The devil knew that God's words could no longer stop him so he flew into Egypt. He got inside the Egyptian Kings. He told the Egyptians that God's people were evil. He made them hate the Israelites. They made them their slaves. He kept God's people in slavery for 400 years. The devil laughed for 400 years. Then he returned to God to see how his gag was holding up. He saw a tear in God's eye. This really made him happy.

The devil leaves again and returns as before.

Narrator   As the devil made fun of God's tear, the Israelites were freed from slavery in Egypt. They were in the Promised Land. The devil left swiftly. He stirred up a war over the whole earth. He led the Babylonians into the homeland of God's people. They killed many of God's people. The Babylonians took the prisoners away from their promised land into their own land called Babylonia. And as they were held prisoner for years and years, the devil laughed. Not one of God's people was left in his or her homeland.

The devil tired of his misery and returned to God. God was crying. The devil was laughing.

God holds up one finger. The devil dances around him.

Narrator   The devil stopped laughing when God held up one finger. He thought lightning would strike him, but nothing happened. The devil danced again. But his curiosity got the best of him. He said: "What is it, God? You want to go higher?" God shook his head, no.

"Are you counting the number of your people left after my wars?" The devil asked. God shook his head no. "Watch, God," said the devil.

The devil waves his arms in sweeping fashion from the altar.

Narrator   "Look, see what I've done to your people now?" He caused another war on God's people. Now they were ruled by the Roman people in all of Judea. They suffered again and again. "Now watch this, God," the devil shouted. "Watch this, one finger only."

The devil waves one finger in a sweeping fashion from the altar.

Narrator   The devil waved his wicked finger and the Romans made God's people pay high taxes to Rome. They had to pay more than they could ever afford. Some of them were whipped for not being able to pay. Many of them were killed for not paying. God's people were very unhappy. They wondered where their God was. He made promises to them. Some of them gave up on God; he hadn't spoken to them for years.

God still had one finger up. "What is it you want, God?" asked the devil. He just had to know. "Do you want me to give you one thing?" God shook his head no. "Do you want me to take the gag off?" asked the devil. God shook his head yes. "Oh no," sneered the devil. "Then you'll speak to the world all your words of love." God shook his head, no. "You won't speak words of love?" asked the devil. "Oh, I get it. You want me to allow you to say one word." God shook his head yes, and yes, and yes. "One word can't hurt, I guess." said the confident devil. "You promise, only one word?" God shook his head again—yes.

Well, the devil saw this as a challenge. He tried to think of the word God might say. He couldn't think of any word that could hurt him. So he laughed and decided to challenge God again; after all, he won the last time and was able to gag God. One word, ha! Surely one word couldn't hurt the devil's rule on Earth.

The devil removes gag and stands there. God mimes as narration indicates.

Narrator   He loosened God's gag. God rubbed his lips and moved his jaw up and down. After all he couldn't speak for a million years. He cleared his throat to be sure that his word could be heard all across the earth. The devil, trying to hold back his laughter, stood next to God.

God slowly stretches out his arms to all the audience. He keeps his arms out to the people until the whole play is over. The devil crouches in pain and quickly exits. Mary and Joseph enter slowly heading for the bale of hay.

Narrator   He watched God raise his arms; they stretched over all the earth and to the ends of heaven.

Narrator Then God spoke a single word. And the devil crouched in awful pain. He ran away from God and hid from his sight. He couldn't stand the word. He even dropped the gag. He couldn't get near God after his word. God's word was so good, so great, so full of God's love for his people that it became a real person, a baby. God's word, a single word, is—Jesus.

Immediately after the word *Jesus* is spoken, the Folk Group leads the audience in singing. They sing the word *Jesus* to the tune of "Silent Night, Holy Night." They keep singing as the rest of the play unfolds. As soon as the word *Jesus* is spoken, Mary sits upon the bale and picks up the baby doll. She rocks it in her lap as Joseph stands next to her. Next, the Shepherds enter to the outside of right stage. The archangel enters behind them and goes to right stage. She extends her arm with the sword to the shepherds. They follow her. She stands behind Mary as the shepherds kneel at random to the right stage side of Joseph. Then, the six or more angels enter. Half enter from right stage while the other half enter from the left. They outstretch their arms and line up next to the archangel behind Mary. Last, the Star Angel enters and goes to left stage. The Three Kings enter behind her and kneel at her feet. She moves next to the angels as the Three Kings rise and kneel at random to the left stage side of Joseph. Singing can now come to a finish.

Special Note See this section in *Only Fifty Feet from Christmas.*

The Drummer Boy, who appears in *Only Fifty Feet from Christmas,* may lead the offertory procession.

The Very First
First Communion

A play for costumed players and mimes of the Last Supper.

Rehearsal Requirement Two hours one day prior to the liturgy with a one-half hour brush-up just before the Mass.

Characters Jesus (a mime in a white alb)
Judas (a mime with one-half of his face white and the other black—See Appendix under Quick Make-Up)
11 Apostles (not mimes—dressed as one would have imagined their dress during the time)
Narrator

Props None

Staging Enter three apostles who go to front stage. They mime a discussion as they look around. One disciple exits as the other two clean up and prepare table setting.

Narrator It was the feast day called Passover and the little town of Jerusalem was very crowded. Jesus sent three of his apostles into the city to rent a room so they could celebrate Passover together. Jesus knew that tonight's Passover would be the first of its kind—a new Passover feast. The three apostles looked and looked. Many rooms were already rented. Finally, they found a room and went in to look around. The place was dirty, but not too dirty. They thought they could have it ready by the time Jesus and the others arrived. Two of them stayed while one went to get the others.

Jesus and the other apostles enter and go to front stage. They stand around in happy discussion. Jesus sits in the center of the front stage and motions for the others to join him. Judas sits at one extreme end. They are all facing the audience.

Narrator The trip was long enough to allow the two apostles to get the room in order. The floor was swept and the table was set. Then, Jesus and the other apostles arrived. They talked about old times. Judas laughed when he heard how one apostle took the wrong turn. He almost got lost down a dark alley. They almost missed the whole Passover party. Finally, when Jesus knew the time was right, he sat at the table. He asked the others to join him. Judas sat at the far end of the table.

They all eat, drink, and enter into lively discussion. All except Judas who eats and stares at Jesus. Jesus stares at him.

Narrator Judas knew that when the celebration was over he would tell the police where Jesus was staying. He wanted them to arrest Jesus. The celebration of Passover began. They ate, and drank, and prayed, and sang songs together. They told jokes and laughed. But not Judas; he stared at Jesus. And Jesus was looking at Judas, knowing what he would do that very night.

Jesus raises his arms and everyone directs their attention to him. Jesus raises bread and the cup, then he passes it around. They all eat and drink while watching Jesus.

Narrator Jesus raised his arms to heaven and prayed. Everyone stopped and watched. This was not the normal way of celebrating Passover. This was something new; something they hadn't done before. Jesus said, "I have greatly desired to eat this Passover with you before I suffer. And I won't eat again until I eat with you at my Father's table in heaven." He then reached across the table and raised a loaf of bread. He broke it in pieces, asked God to bless it, and gave it to them to eat. He said, "Take this and eat it, this is my body." But they didn't understand what he meant.

One of them was about to ask Jesus a question when Jesus raised his cup of wine. He asked God to bless it and said, "Take this and drink it, this is my blood." The question was forgotten and they all drank.

Jesus looks at Judas. Others argue heatedly. Jesus listens to Judas as the others continue to argue. All become quiet as Jesus passes the plate of food from one to the other until it reaches Judas. Judas eats and exits swiftly.

Narrator Jesus spoke again, "I tell you solemnly, one of you will hand me over to the police tonight." They started to argue, "Is it you? It's not me. Is it him?" Judas didn't argue. Over the shouting, Judas asked Jesus who it might be. And Jesus passed a dish with a bit of food on it to Judas. As Judas ate, Jesus said, "It is the one who eats from this dish." Judas stood up and ran out of the room. Jesus quietly said to him as he left, "Be quick about what you are to do."

Apostles quiet down and look to Jesus. Jesus stands and steps back a few steps. With his hands stretched out he speaks to the apostles.

Narrator The apostles thought Judas was going to pay the rent for the room; after all he was their money holder. Jesus rose up again. The apostles watched as Jesus again changed their normal Passover celebration. One apostle even said, "This Passover meal celebration is certainly different. It's the first of its kind. We are in communion with each other and Jesus more so now than last year's celebration. It's kind of a new communion; a First Communion." Then Jesus spoke: "Now is the Son of Man glorified and God is glorified in him."

Jesus steps forward and goes to the audience. His arms are out to the audience as he moves about them touching some on their shoulders.

Narrator My children, I am not to be with you much longer. You will look for me, but I say to you now what I once said to the people; "Where I am going, you cannot come. I give you a new commandment: Love one another. Such as my love has been for you, so must your love be for each other."

Jesus returns to front stage. His apostles stand and gather around him. He raises his arms to the audience again and they all exit.

Narrator   "This is how all will know you for my disciples: by your love for one another."

Puppets are used with the puppet stage described on pages 90-93.

Hail, Mary

A play for puppets on the Annunciation.

Rehearsal Requirement Two hours.

Characters Woman's Voice
(Puppets)
Mary
Angel
Joseph
Elizabeth
Father (the high priest of the village)

Props None

Staging See Appendix; Puppet Stage Construction

Mary, Joseph, and Father pop up at right stage. Mary and Joseph are together while Father stands in front of them.

Father	Well, Mary and Joseph, the first step is about to begin. You will now become engaged. Joseph, did you bring the engagement rings?
Joseph	Yes, Father. Here is Mary's. Here's mine.
Father	Both of you hold the rings up for the blessing.
	Mary and Joseph raise their arms.
Father	O God of Israel, bless these engagement rings for Joseph and Mary. Let your grace be with them as they will be engaged for one year. You may wear the rings now and love one another no matter how tough the world becomes for you. God bless you.
	They place them on and embrace.
Mary	Joseph, we are finally engaged. And in one short year we will be married.
Joseph	I must go into the city with Father. I'll meet you at your house for supper, okay?
Mary	That's fine, Joseph. I'll be by the stream until supper is ready. Goodbye, Father, and thank you for blessing our engagement rings. I know God will be with us until we are married.
Father and Joseph	Goodbye, Mary.
	Father and Joseph drop behind stage. Mary walks to the stream, where she lies down.
Mary	What a lovely day it's going to be. Hello you big mountains across the stream. My boyfriend and I are engaged to be married. My ring looks like your snowcaps; white and beautiful. I think I'll take a nap by your stream if you don't mind.
Woman's Voice	Mary. Mary.
Mary	Yes ma'am
Woman's Voice	Don't go too far; supper is almost ready. Your father will be home from work soon.
Mary	Okay, I'll be resting by the stream. Oh, and Joseph will be eating with us tonight. We have a surprise to tell you.
Woman's Voice	That's nice. I'll set another place for that good boy, Joseph. He's always welcomed in our house. You ought to think about getting engaged to that boy. You've been seeing him a lot lately. Well, don't go too far away, you hear?
Mary	Okay. I'll be able to hear you. Oh, how tired I am. Now to take a nap by this cool stream. Ahhhh.
	Angel pops up at mountains. He looks to the left stage, then right, where he sees Mary. He comes next to her. She awakens rubbing her eyes. Then she crouches in fear. She rises after the angel calms her.
Angel	There I made it—all the way from heaven. Oh, I must be a little off target. Let's see, where is that girl? Ah, there she is, resting by God's stream. "Hail, Mary, full of grace!"

Mary	What? Sir, you scared me.
Angel	Don't be afraid, Mary—I am an angel from heaven. God sent me to you. I am his messenger. You have made God very happy. You will soon have a baby boy. He will be God's Son and his name will be Jesus. "Great will be his dignity and he will be called Son of the Most High. The Lord God will give him the throne of David his father. He will rule over the house of Jacob forever and his reign will be without end."
Mary	But sir, I am only engaged. I am not married. How can I have a baby?
Angel	God can do anything. Nothing is too hard or too difficult for God. He will send his Holy Spirit down and you will have a baby boy. He will be called the Son of God. Even your old cousin, Elizabeth, is going to have a baby boy soon. You see, nothing is impossible with God.
Mary	(Bowing) Sir, I love God very much. Please tell God I will do it. I will have the baby boy that will be Jesus, Son of God. I am his Servant.
Angel	(Slowly dropping behind stage.) "Hail, Mary, full of grace! The Lord is with you. Blessed are you among women."
	Mary stays bowed a few seconds, then rises quickly and moves to right stage.
Woman's Voice	Mary. Supper's ready.
Mary	(Looking down at house) Mother, you'll never guess what's happened. I saw an angel. I'm going to have the Son of God. Pack my suitcase; I'm going to see my cousin, Elizabeth. She's going to have a baby boy, too.
Woman's Voice	What, that old woman, have a baby? That'll be a miracle.
	Mary drops behind stage as Joseph pops up between the stream and mountains. He goes to right stage.
Joseph	Wow, what a party! I don't think I'll be able to eat a thing at Mary's. I'll still go, just to be with her. Let's see, I can jump this stream about here.
	Mary pops up at right stage and runs to Joseph.
Mary	Joseph, Joseph, I have the most wonderful news!
Joseph	What is it, Mary? You certainly are excited.
Mary	An angel from God came to me and told me I would have a baby boy soon. He'll be the Son of God.
Joseph	What! You can't have a baby. We're not married yet. We're only engaged. Did you marry someone else?
Mary	No, Joseph. Don't be so foolish. It's God's Son. We can still get married.
Joseph	If you're not married and going to have a baby our law says you are sinful. You will be killed. The punishment for that is to be stoned until you are dead.
	Mary weeps.
Joseph	Go ahead and cry. I'm not marrying you anymore. You must be lying. Who

will believe a story like that. The Son of God indeed. Goodbye, Mary. I must speak to the high priest about this.

Joseph walks to right stage and drops behind stage. Mary weeps then goes over the mountains to Elizabeth's house. Elizabeth pops up at left stage to greet Mary.

Mary   I won't cry anymore, God. It is your Son to be borne by me and I know you'll take care of us. I'll continue over the mountains to my cousin Elizabeth. I hope she doesn't hate me when I tell her the good news.

Elizabeth   Mary, Mary, I knew you would come. (Embracing Mary) "Blessed are you among women and blessed is the fruit of your womb, Jesus."

Mary   I'm so glad you don't hate me.

Elizabeth   Hate you? The Mother of us all. Never!

Mary   But wait till you hear my good news.

Elizabeth   I know. The angel visited me too. You are having a baby boy who is God's Son.

Mary   Yes, that's right (embracing her again).

Elizabeth   And the Angel told me that I will have a baby boy, too. My son will be called, John. He will tell all the people about Jesus. He will prepare the way for God's Son. Come, I'll help you unpack. How long will you be staying?

Mary   (as they both drop behind stage.) About three months or so . . .

(Joseph pops up at stream. Father pops up at right stage. Joseph goes to him.)

Joseph   Father, Father.

Father   Yes, Joseph, what is it?

Joseph   Bad news. Mary has told me that she is going to have a baby.

Father   Oh no! The law is very direct. If this is true, and she's not married, she will be judged and probably killed.

Joseph   But Father, I still love her. But I can't marry her now.

Father   She will be taken to court for this. Where is she?

Joseph   There's more bad news.

Father   More? What? Is it worse?

Joseph   Yes. She says that her baby will be the Son of God.

Father   She's lying! That kind of storytelling is crazy. The people will not only kill her, but they'll hate you and her family. She must not say a word about this.

Joseph   Father, Mary has never lied before. I almost believe her.

Father   Joseph, only you can save her. If you were to marry her tonight, everything would be okay. But if I were you, I wouldn't do it. If the people ever find out, they will kill you too.

Joseph   I'll have to go for a walk to think. Maybe we can help her out of town. She could go away, to another country. But I'd miss her. What am I to do?

Father drops behind stage as Joseph walks back to the stream. Angel pops up at mountains. He goes to Joseph, who is sleeping. Joseph gets up.

Joseph   Wow, what a rotten day this has turned into. (yawning) I think I'll take a nap by this stream.

Angel   Ouch, off target again. There's Joseph. Does he need help! Poor Joseph, I'll help him. ''Joseph, Son of David, have no fear.''

Joseph   What! Who are you?

Angel   I am an angel sent from God. Do not be afraid to marry Mary. She will have a baby soon. And it is God's Son. She loves you and needs you now more than ever. If you love your God and Mary, you will marry her.

Angel drops behind stage. Mary pops up at left stage. She walks over the mountains to Joseph.

Joseph   What? Where did the angel go? Did I really see an angel from God? Did he talk to me?

Mary   Hello, Joseph. I've just come home from my cousin's house in the hill country. How have you been? Please don't hate me anymore.

Joseph   Mary, I love you! I've seen God's angel! He told me what to do! It's what I wanted to do all along. We will be married tonight! And I'll take care of God's Son until he becomes a man. Let's go quickly.

Mary   But Joseph, what about the high priest?

Joseph   You will be a married woman tomorrow. God will take care of us. All we have to do is be happy that God's Son is coming into the world. It is what our people have been waiting for for hundreds of years. Jesus is coming! Think of it, we have been chosen to be the family of God's Son. Let's go!

Mary   I'm tired from my long journey. I'll rest here by the stream. You take my suitcase and go ahead. You take care of the final arrangements with the high priest. And be sure to tell my mother and father that I'll be along shortly.

Joseph   Okay, Mary. But don't be too long.

Mary sleeps by the stream. The angel pops up at the mountains. He raises his arms to Mary and drops behind stage.

Mary   I'm so sleepy. I'll just rest for a minute.

Angel   ''Hail, Mary, full of grace! The Lord is with you. Blessed are you among women. And blessed is the fruit of your womb, Jesus.''

Woman's Voice   Mary. Mary.

Mary   (awakening and running to right stage where she drops behind stage) Yes, ma'am. I'm coming. Me and God's Son are coming home.

Appendix

BULLETIN INSERTS

These serve several purposes:
a. To inform children not enrolled in the parish school or CCD of a future children's liturgy.
b. To enable adults to decide to attend or to attend an earlier Mass.
c. To make the whole parish aware of the concern for the children.

These inserts can be done easily and inexpensively. Divide a ditto or stencil spirit master in half as the sample shows. On one side design a cover sheet appealing to children; it need not be professional. On the other side, type your information, both for adults and children. Say enough, but not too much. Tease the children with a gift presentation (see Handouts). Type and draw whatever it takes to get them there. Once they experience the liturgy, you'll see the value of good, attractive advertisement.

By using this type of insert design, you need only run off one-half of your desired number. After one printing is complete, you will have a stack of paper printed on one side only. Flip the stack over in the feed tray and run them through the stencil machine again, making sure that the cover sheet prints on the back of the typed sheet. After this run, merely cut your stack in half and insert them into your bulletin.

I cannot emphasize enough the importance of typing only just what needs to be said. There is a tendency to want to tell everyone all about the event. We've learned it is not needed. The less said, the better.

INVITATIONS

The purpose of these is to make the children feel special, that it is their liturgy, and to remind them of their liturgy as close as possible to the liturgy date.

Have the school and CCD teachers hand these to their students on the last day of classes just prior to the liturgy date.

The invitations can be made easily and inexpensively. Divide a ditto or stencil spirit master in quarters as the sample shows. In the top two rectangles, design your cover sheet; keep it simple. In the bottom two rectangles, type your invitation to the children in simple childlike language. Again, if you are just beginning, it is wise to mention the gift (see Handouts).

By using this type of invitation design, you need only run off one quarter of your desired number. After one printing is complete, you will have a stack of paper printed on only one side. Flip the stack over in the feed tray and run them through the stencil machine again, making sure that the cover sheets print on the back of the typed sheets. After this run, merely cut your stack in quarters and deliver them to the teachers. The children love receiving invitations to parties and their own liturgies.

When their parents see the pains you have taken and the enthusiasm you have, they will make sure their children attend. Once they experience the child's joy in celebrating the liturgy, they'll be back again and again. And they'll come back as much for themselves as for their children.

HANDOUTS

This is intended to give the children an opportunity to carry the Mass home with them. It is also to encourage them to seek help from their parents to appreciate the theme.

I have found the best handout is a book type. Use an 8½'' x 11'' sheet of paper that folds lengthwise. This gives you four pages that measure 8½'' x 5½''. The first page is your cover and theme statement. You can fill it with dot to dot, fill in the blanks, etc. But it must always be about the gospel play and theme. The last page is for parent participation. Whatever you type or draw here, make it too difficult for the child to do alone. The inside pages should be coloring pages that allow them to create what they experience from the liturgy.

The handout can be drawn on two 8½'' x 11'' ditto or stencil spirit masters. Always run off more than you think you may need. There is nothing worse than a child with his or her hand out at the altar, and you have nothing to give. An alternate to this format is a two-sided handout similiar to the bulletin insert.

QUICK MAKE-UP FOR MIMES AND CLOWNS

Materials needed: paper towels, theatrical cold cream, clown white, masquerade stick make-up, mascara.

1. Apply a thin layer of cold cream to the face. Mimes need only cover just above the eyebrows and around the cheeks in an oval to the bottom of the chin. Clowns should do their whole face. Cold cream is very useful for cleanup.

2. Apply a thin layer of clown white. Place a small amount on your fingertips and spread it around your face. Do the eyelids, eyebrows, about the nostrils. Mimes should have only an oval shape just above the eyebrows to the bottom of the chin. Clowns should do their whole face.

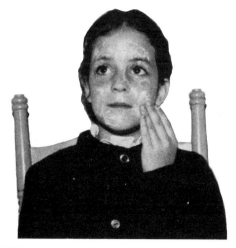

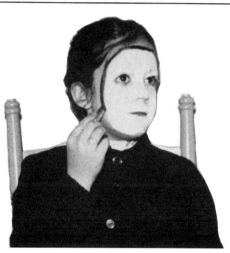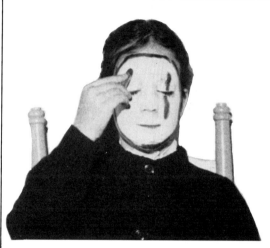

3. Stick make-up is used as follows after the clown white:

Mimes—Use the black make-up stick to draw a single black line on the outside of the oval. It is to just touch the white. Then draw one vertical line from just above the eyebrow down over the eyelid to the middle of the cheek on both sides.

Clowns—Use the colored make-up sticks. Use red around the lips. Make a wide red mouth and outline it with the mascara eyeliner stick. If you do other colored designs about your eyes or cheeks, outline them with the mascara stick.

4. Cleanup with paper towels only. Do not use water. The oil based make-up will slide off onto the paper towel because of the cold cream base. Then use more cold cream to clean off any make-up still remaining in the corners of your eyes or in your eyebrows. Once this is complete, you can wash with soap and water.

These materials can be purchased at a novelty store. They are inexpensive (one 16 oz. tin of clown white will last two years or more). If you cannot locate a shop, you might write to a manufacturer.

MIME DRESS

Mime dress is always dark—black or blue. Dark jeans and a black long sleeve shirt work very well. If one of the characters is Jesus let him also wear a white T-shirt over his black shirt. All mimes wear black socks and perform without shoes.

RECRUITING

The plays are best performed by eighth graders, and older, with some younger children mixed in, as low as second graders.

The plays are best narrated by adults. The spoken words are the most important part of the scripts and need to be read with confidence and cadence. Unless you have an exceptional child reader, use adult readers.

Recruiting children to perform as a mime is easy. Merely visit the parish school and CCD classes dressed in mime make-up. Expect to begin with only a few. Once the liturgy takes place, you'll be turning them away; that has been my experience. One school teacher allowed her eighth graders to earn extra credit for being involved with our children's liturgies.

As an added incentive, take pictures of the mime and give them to the actresses and actors during school time. Interest will be generated by the photos themselves.

During rehearsals, act like a professional director; wear a weird hat, bring a "director's" chair. Allow a five-minute "laugh time" break at the beginning of rehearsal. Use stage talk; "okay, action," "Cut," "very good, baby," "roll 'em," "sweetheart," etc. This puts the children at ease just before you must get serious. Don't expect great rehearsals. I haven't had a successful one yet; but all of our performances have been great. There's magic when it's showtime. They call it magic, I know it's the Spirit.

Begin Mass with a brief prayer with the mimes. End Mass with an announced "cast party." Believe me, when the word gets out, you'll never look for volunteers again. As a matter of fact, we now have our own mime troupe, *Yours, Mime, and Ours,* with a membership of 35 children from second grade to twelfth.

And be prepared to fall in love with all of your mimes. It's unavoidable, and a great feeling!

PUPPET STAGE CONSTRUCTION

This stage is inexpensive and stores easily. It is quickly constructed and lends itself to all types of scenery design. It allows a roomy area for the puppeteers to work from and enables them to be able to read from scripts rather than memorizing; scripts can be stuck to the stage itself. Refer to the drawing for these directions.

Materials needed: 1 – 4' x 8' piece of paneling, 3 – 2'' x 2'' x 8' pieces of lumber, 2 – 1'' x 3'' x 4' pieces of lumber, 2 hinges, 2 large pieces of cardboard, and 1 can of flat black paint.

1. Cut one of the 2 x 2's in half. Make a 4' x 8' frame on the floor by nailing them together at the corners.

2. Lay the 4' x 8' paneling on the frame, finished side up, and nail it to the frame; raise it up.

3. Screw the hinges to one end of the 1' x 3' pieces of lumber and attach it to each top corner of the 4' x 8' frame on the inside of the stage, forming two legs.

4. Let the stage lean back on the 1 x 3's at your desired angle and secure it with a piece of string, so that the legs will not slip out. Cut the cardboard to fit these leg triangles and secure it with string to the legs and stage. This hides the puppeteers from children peeking around the sides.

5. Paint everything that shows outside toward the audience flat black.

6. Untie the cardboard triangles and fold in the legs for a storage requirement of 4' x 8' x 3''.

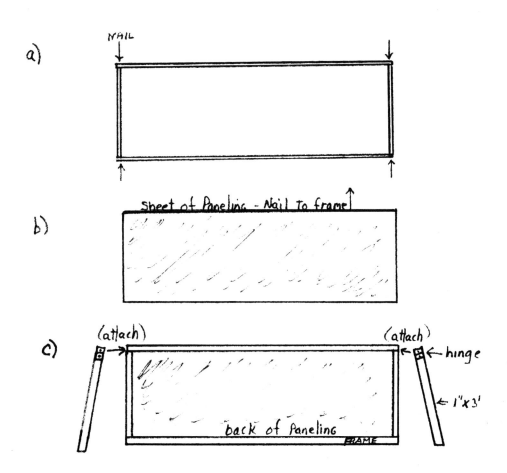

d)

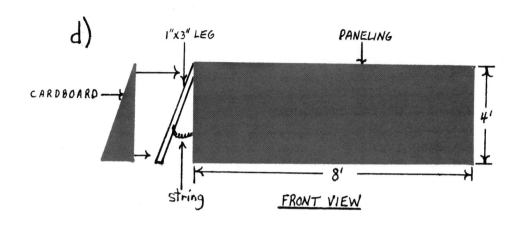

1"x3" LEG

PANELING

CARDBOARD

4'

8'

string

FRONT VIEW

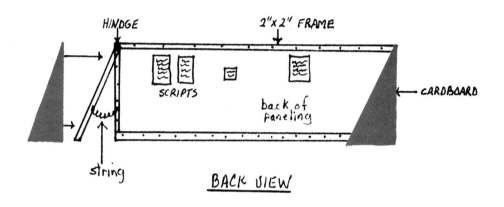

HINGE

2"x2" FRAME

SCRIPTS

back of paneling

CARDBOARD

string

BACK VIEW

STAGE WITH SCENERY
OF WHITE POSTER BOARD

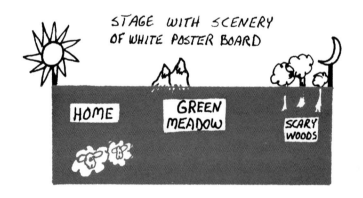

HOME

GREEN MEADOW

SCARY WOODS

A RECORD OF CELEBRATIONS

The following table might be used to record useful information. By keeping a record of the celebrations you have used, the date, who it was intended for, and the time it was held, suggestions for improve-ment, the names of the celebrant(s) and other personnel, the songs used — you have taken a concrete step toward more effective celebrations.

Date/time	Title of Celebration	Intended Audience	Names of Personnel	Songs Used	Suggestions/ Comments

Date/time	Title of Celebration	Intended Audience	Names of Personnel	Songs Used	Suggestions/ Comments

Date/time	Title of Celebration	Intended Audience	Names of Personnel	Songs Used	Suggestions/ Comments

DeAngelis, William

Acting Out the Gospels